W9-BBM-321

OUR FRAGILE PLANET

SHRINKING FORESTS

Jenny Tesar

Series Editor:
Bernard S. Cayne

A Blackbirch Graphics Book

Facts On File
New York • Oxford

Facts On File, Inc.
460 Park Avenue South
New York, NY 10016
USA

Facts On File Limited
Collins Street
Oxford OX4 1XJ
United Kingdom

Library of Congress Cataloging-in-Publication Data
Tesar, Jenny E.
    Shrinking forests.
    (Our fragile planet; 3/by Jenny Elizabeth Tesar; series editor, Bernard S. Cayne.)
    Includes bibliographical references and index.
    Summary: Explores the crucial role of the forest ecosystem and how its invaluable resources are endangered by pollution, development, and lack of careful observation.
    ISBN 0-8160-2492-8
    1. Forest ecology—Juvenile literature. 2. Forest conservation—Juvenile literature. 3. Deforestation—Juvenile literature. [1. Forest ecology. 2. Forest conservation. 3. Ecology.] I. Title. II. Series: Tesar, Jenny E. Our fragile planet; 3.
QH541.5.F6T47 1991
333.75—dc20   90-47191

A British CIP catalogue record for this book is available from the British Library

Facts On File Books are available at special discounts when purchased in bulk quantities for businesses, associations, institutions or sales promotions. Please call our Special Sales Department in New York at 212/683-2244 (dial 800/322-8755 except in NY, AK, or HI) or in Oxford at 865/728399.

Design: Blackbirch Graphics, Inc.

Printed and Manufactured in the United States of America.

10 9 8 7 6 5 4 3 2 1

This book is printed on acid-free paper.

CONTENTS

1
DISAPPEARING FORESTS

 A minute is a very brief moment of time. For the world's forests, however, there are too many minutes. Each minute means the disappearance of another huge chunk of forest. Each minute means the death of trees hundreds of years old, plus the death of scores of animals that depended on those trees for food and shelter.

As the 1990s began, the world's forests were disappearing at the rate of 80 acres (32 hectares) a minute. Each year, 40 million to 50 million acres (16–20 million hectares) were being wiped out. That's an area more than six times the size of Maryland, an area about the size of the state of Washington.

Minutes quickly add up to years. Years add up to decades. Between 1970 and 1990, the Earth lost more than 500 million acres (202 million hectares) of forests—an area about the size of the United States east of the Mississippi. This alarming loss of forests is occurring all over the world.

In North America, the most serious losses are occurring in Oregon, Washington and British Columbia. Controversial lumbering practices are clearing vast areas of tall Douglas firs. For 200 years or more, these trees survived fires, windstorms, floods and other natural calamities. But it takes little more than a minute for a person wielding a chainsaw to bring one of these giants crashing to the ground—to be turned into paper bags, diapers, drinking cups and other products.

Opposite page: Destructive lumbering practices are causing the most serious losses of forest around the world.

In Europe, it isn't the lumbering industry that is destroying the forests. Rather, pollution from human activities is killing forests that for centuries have been praised by poets and musicians. Needles on pines and firs turn yellow, then fall from the branches, leaving behind skeletons that gradually turn gray. A handmade sign erected alongside a German forest pointed out one of the problems: *Autos Töten Wälder*. Cars Kill Forests.

The most serious losses are occurring in the tropics. Here, rapidly growing populations of poor people, trying simply to survive, cut trees for firewood and clear plots on which to raise crops. Here, too, commercial operations cut vast areas to meet the ever-growing global demand for lumber, paper and other forest products. Ranchers burn forests to raise cattle, producing meat that is exported to North America. Miners strip the land to extract iron and other minerals.

Why Should We Care?

Forests are among our most valuable resources. People depend on trees for fuel, food, medicine and rubber. Wood from trees is used to build homes and furniture, make paper and rayon, and manufacture hundreds of chemical products. People also use forests for recreational activities such as camping, hiking, picnicking and fishing.

Forests are much, much more than a source of products or pleasure, however. They are home for millions of kinds, or species, of plants and animals. Each of these species is unique—different in some way from every other species. This biological diversity, or variety, is of immense importance to human beings. "Like mountaineers roped together on a steep cliff, we depend utterly on the survival of other species," wrote G. Jon Roush, former chairman of the Nature Conservancy's board of governors. As Roush pointed out, almost half of all the medicines we use are derived from other species. The future of our food supplies depends on improving domestic crops by breeding them with related wild plants.

When people cut down forests, animals become homeless and face a shortage of food. Once pandas roamed through forests that covered much of China. Deforestation has confined the pandas to ever-shrinking areas. These areas are too small to support many pandas. There is only enough bamboo—the only food that pandas will eat—to feed a small population of the animals. When animal populations shrink, it becomes difficult for the animals to find mates and reproduce. The animals die without producing a new generation. Eventually, the species ceases to exist. It becomes extinct.

As a result of deforestation, an unprecedented number of species are becoming extinct. "The extinction rate is over 150 species a day," estimated William Mansfield, deputy director of the United Nations Environment Program, in 1990. "Biological diversity faces the worst stage of mass extinction in 65 million years." Many species are being destroyed before scientists are able to identify and classify them. They are disappearing from Earth without our knowledge of their existence, their beauty, their potential value. Deforestation also affects climate. The loss of forests, particularly tropical rain forests, changes local weather. This, in turn, could change global climate. Also, trees limit the amount of carbon dioxide in the atmosphere by absorbing it. As forests shrink, increasing concentrations of carbon dioxide in the atmosphere are expected to cause significant increases in world temperatures.

As forests are cut, erosion increases. Without tree roots to hold the soil in place, water quickly runs off the land, carrying the soil with it. Downstream, there may be severe flooding. In Asia, for example, deforestation in the Himalayas has resulted in thousands of deaths from flooding in India and Bangladesh.

Can the Forests Be Saved?

In recent years, people have become more aware of the many important roles played by forests. They increasingly recognize that their well-being and the well-being of planet Earth are threatened by dwindling forests. If we are to save the world's remaining forests, we need to deal with the causes of deforestation. First, we must deal with direct causes. That is, we must find ways to slow and reverse destruction due to pollution, overcutting by the timber industry and clearing for farms and ranches. Second, we must deal with indirect causes, particularly poverty and the population explosion.

Massive reforestation programs can turn now-barren hills and valleys into new forests. These new forests will not have the wonderful diversity of life found in the Earth's virgin forests. But they will help fulfill people's needs for fuel, lumber and other products. And they will relieve pressure to destroy those wild forests that are particularly rich in giant trees, endangered species and other valued organisms.

Too often, the multiple values of forests have been ignored in the rush to cut timber, create ranches, build roads or extract mineral resources. This shortsighted view can be changed, particularly if governments stress the need for better management practices. One essential goal is sustained yield, that is, the amount of timber harvested should not be greater than the growth rate of the forest. Additionally, large tracts of forests can be set aside as national parks and preserves.

A reduced demand for timber can also help conserve forests. Helpful actions include increased recycling of paper, making more efficient use of lumber in construction, employing more efficient wood stoves and better utilizing lumber remnants. Better pollution controls and conservation of fossil fuels can help limit acid rain and other airborne causes of forest death.

Where rapid population growth is a basic factor in deforestation, populations need to be stabilized at levels that can be supported by available resources. Fairer distribution of agricultural land and other resources may also be necessary. For example, in Latin America 7% of the landowners own 93% of the farmland. Most of this farmland is used to raise crops that are exported and are sold for money. The remaining 7% of the farmable land cannot produce enough food for the millions of poor people. The people are forced to cut down forests in an effort to grow enough food to avoid starvation. As The World Commission on Environment and Development pointed out in its 1987 report, "the population issue is not solely about numbers. . .threats to the sustainable use of resources come as much from inequalities in people's access to resources and from the ways in which they use them as from the sheer numbers of people."

Developed countries with comparatively high living standards can provide technological and financial help to poorer countries. They can limit their exploitation of the poorer countries' resources. And they can conserve their own resources. There is an old saying: Actions speak louder than words. Poor countries cannot be expected to accept criticism from rich countries that continue to pursue wasteful practices. Jay D. Hair, president of the National Wildlife Federation, wrote: "Americans have begun to speak out against the burning of the rain forests . . . the loss of which threatens our very existence. But our call for reform falls flat in the face of continuing attacks on our own ancient forests. We are preaching a double standard."

Shridath S. Ramphal, chairman of the West Indian Commission noted, "If the United States cannot muster the political courage to stop the environmental damage caused by cheap gasoline (or, for that matter, by cutting down the temperate rain forest of Alaska), it is not difficult to understand why governments in more politically fragile societies also fail to act."

The forests can survive. They can continue to cleanse the Earth's air and moderate its climate. Their many fascinating creatures can prosper and be a continuing source of products and pleasure. But people everywhere must make the survival of these organisms a central goal in their lives. This needs to be done not at some distant, unspecified time, but now. Each day that individuals, communities and nations procrastinate, another 40 million to 50 million acres (16–20 million hectares) of forest disappear.

Saving the Earth's forests and replacing those that have been destroyed will not be easy to achieve. But the fate of the forests may well be the fate of human beings.

THE PEOPLE THREAT

By 1990, an estimated 5.3 billion people lived on the Earth. The number of births is far greater than the number of deaths, so the population grows rapidly. At the start of the decade, three babies were born every second every day. There were a quarter of a million new people.

Most population growth is occurring in tropical areas. The United Nations predicts that the world's population will reach 6.25 billion by 2000 and 8.47 billion by 2025. Almost all the growth—95%—will occur in the developing countries of Africa, Asia and Latin America. Coupled with poverty, population growth is responsible for much deforestation. "When both agricultural and nonagricultural needs are taken into account, growing populations may be responsible for as much as 80% of the loss of forest cover," indicated Nafis Sadik, executive director of the United Nations Population Fund.

2

TREES AND FORESTS

In autumn, an acorn falls from a tall white oak. The acorn is about as big as the tip of a person's thumb. It lies on the ground only a brief time before it is picked up by a squirrel. The squirrel carries it away from the parent tree and buries it in soil, planning to return at some later time to enjoy a tasty meal. But the squirrel forgets about the acorn. With the coming spring, the acorn sprouts. In time the seedling will grow into a tree 75 feet (23 meters) tall, with a trunk more than 4 feet (1.2 meters) in diameter, thousands of beautiful green leaves and its own crop of acorns.

What Is a Tree?

Oaks, pines, maples, cherries, birches, willows, cedars, palms, hemlocks, figs, hickories, elms, mahoganies, apples, eucalyptuses—there are several thousand kinds, or species, of trees. They have different sizes, shapes, barks, leaves and seeds. But they all share certain characteristics.

Trees are woody plants with a single main stem called the trunk. The trunk rises from the root system and supports branches and leaves.

The root system has two important functions. It anchors the tree in the ground, and it absorbs water and nutrients from the soil. These nutrients are conducted through the trunk to the crown. The crown consists of branches and

Opposite page:
Trees are adapted to the environments in which they live. Spruce and fir trees that thrive in cold mountainous regions would die if transplanted to a tropical rain forest.

11

leaves. Its upper surface may be 100 feet (30 meters) or more above the soil. The leaves make food for the tree, in a process called photosynthesis. Much of this food, as well as huge amounts of water, are stored in the trunk.

It is interesting to note that tree roots and stems grow in length from the tip only. Thus, if a person drives a nail into the trunk of a young tree at a point 5 feet (1.5 meters) above the ground, then returns 20 years later, that nail will still be 5 feet (1.5 meters) above the ground, though the tree may have tripled in height.

The Wood

A cross section of a tree trunk or branch shows that it consists of five circular layers. The outermost layer, the bark, is composed of dead cells. It insulates the tree and protects the inner, living layers against insect enemies. Immediately inside the bark is the phloem. The phloem carries food from the leaves to the rest of the tree. Eventually phloem dies and becomes part of the bark. The third layer is the cambium. The cells in this very thin layer divide to produce phloem cells on the outer side and xylem cells on the inner side. In this way, the trunk or branch gets wider each year.

Xylem—which is also called sapwood—carries water and nutrients from the roots to the leaves. As the innermost xylem cells die, they form heartwood. Heartwood is the central core of the trunk or branch. In a mature tree, it is the largest part of the trunk. Although heartwood is dead, it provides strength and helps support the tree.

THIS TREE HAS KNEES

Most trees live on dry land. But the bald cypress has an unusual adaptation that enables it to live in swamps. It has big, knobby knees. These cone-shaped structures consist of light, spongy wood. They grow upward from the roots, rising as much as 10 feet (3 meters) above the shallow water. A single tree may have many knees, ranging from a few inches to several feet in height. Some of the knees grow close to the trunk of the tree. Others may be as far as several feet away.

The purpose of the knees is unclear. The most popular theory proposes that the knees provide the submerged roots with oxygen. Exactly how this might occur is not yet known, however. Forests of bald cypresses are found in swamps and rivers of the southeastern United States, in the Mississippi Valley and in Mexico.

Kinds of Trees

Trees are classified in two broad groups: cone-bearing trees and flowering trees.

Pines, spruces, firs and hemlocks are examples of cone-bearing trees, or conifers. Their seeds are produced in cones. Most conifers have narrow leaves, commonly called needles. Most are evergreen. Evergreens shed their needles a few at a time, so that the branches are never bare. Larch is an example of a conifer that drops all its needles in autumn. The bald cypress is another conifer that is not evergreen.

The lumbering industry often refers to the wood of conifers as softwood. The wood is generally lighter and softer than that of flowering trees. Maples, oaks, hickories and beeches are examples of flowering trees. Their seeds are enclosed in a fruit, which is formed from a flower. The leaves are commonly flat and broad. Generally, these trees are deciduous, that is, they shed their leaves in the autumn and grow new leaves the following spring. In tropical climates, however, the leaves of many deciduous species remain on the trees all year. The wood of deciduous trees is often dense and heavy. It is referred to as hardwood. There are exceptions. Some species, including aspen and basswood, have relatively soft wood.

Life Spans

Trees have long life spans. Many species commonly live for hundreds of years. Douglas firs live to be 400 years old. Some bald cypresses live more than 1,000 years. The oldest trees are bristlecone pines in the White Mountains of California. Some of these pines are more than 4,500 years old!

Scientists determine the age of a tree by counting its annual rings. These are the layers of xylem in the trunk. They can be seen by examining a cross section of the trunk. Each year, the cambium produces a new layer of xylem. The thickness of this layer varies from year to year and even from season to season. In early spring, many wide and large vessels are formed. This spring wood appears open and porous when viewed under a microscope. In contrast, summer wood contains fewer vessels and has a denser appearance.

Some annual rings are quite wide; others are very narrow. The differences result from changing environmental conditions. For example, annual rings formed when rainfall is abundant are usually wider than those formed during years of drought. Small trees growing in the shade of larger trees generally have narrow annual rings. When the large trees fall or are cut down, more sunlight reaches the small trees. They produce more food, and the new annual rings are wider.

By examining the annual rings of a tree, scientists can learn interesting facts about the history of the tree and about weather conditions of long ago. In British Columbia, forests filled with thousand-year-old cedars are being logged. By examining the annual rings of these cedars, scientists can learn about environmental conditions in the Pacific Northwest during the days of Leif Eriksson, Christopher Columbus, the American Revolution and other historical periods.

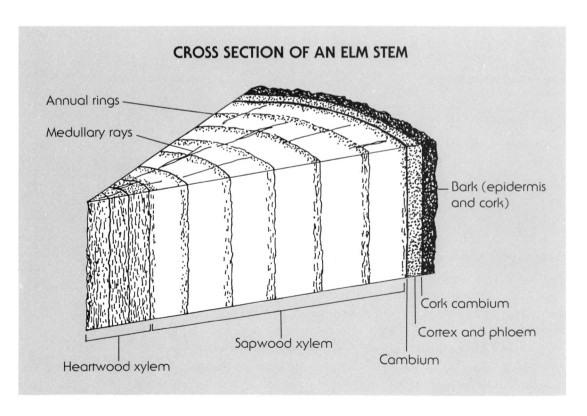

CROSS SECTION OF AN ELM STEM

Annual rings

Medullary rays

Bark (epidermis and cork)

Cork cambium

Cortex and phloem

Cambium

Sapwood xylem

Heartwood xylem

A TREE'S LIFE HISTORY

Most trees in temperate regions grow a new layer of wood each year. When the trunk is cut, these layers can be seen as rings. From these *annual rings*, the tree's life story can be read.

For example, the pine log in this drawing has 72 rings, showing that the tree lived for 72 years.

Narrow center rings indicate that in its early development, the young tree was deprived of sun and rain by older, taller trees.

Wider outer rings indicate that surrounding trees were eventually removed, allowing this tree more access to moisture and sunlight.

Differences in the width of the rings is caused mainly by varying yearly rainfall.

Wider rings on one side indicate the tree was bent in that direction. More wood grew on that side to keep it from falling.

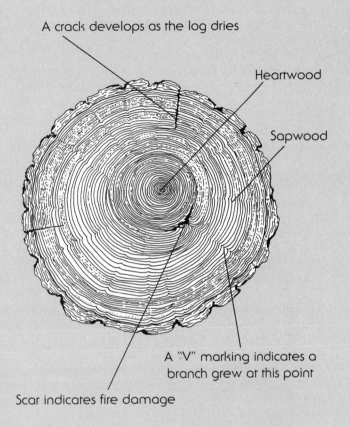

A crack develops as the log dries

Heartwood

Sapwood

A "V" marking indicates a branch grew at this point

Scar indicates fire damage

It is not necessary to cut down a tree to determine its age or to study the history of its growth. Scientists can use a borer to remove a thin core of wood from the trunk. The core is placed under a microscope to magnify the rings and make them easier to count. In a tree such as an ancient bristlecone pine, the rings are extremely thin because the tree grows very slowly. It may take a bristlecone pine 100 years to grow 1 inch (2.5 centimeters) wider.

Kinds of Forests

The kind of forest found in a particular location depends on several environmental factors. These include climatic factors, particularly temperature and moisture. Trees that thrive in warm tropical forests would soon die if transplanted to the Canadian Rockies, where winter temperatures drop far below the freezing point. Similarly, a spruce that prospers in the Rockies would die if transplanted to the Amazon.

Trees vary greatly in their water needs, too. Some can survive in near-desert conditions. Others grow only when their roots are submerged in water. Both the total amount of precipitation and the distribution of this precipitation through the year are important. Generally, the most varied and most luxuriant forests grow in areas where temperatures remain high throughout the year and precipitation is frequent and abundant.

As altitude increases, temperatures steadily decrease. Essentially, each 1,000 feet (305 meters) of ascent equals a 300-mile (483-kilometer) trip toward the polar region. This explains why forests atop the Blue Ridge Mountains of western Virginia are much more like forests in parts of Canada than like forests in nearby low-lying areas of Virginia.

At high mountain elevations and in other exposed positions, wind may be an influencing factor. Strong winds can bend and twist trees. Winds also cause trees to increase the rate at which they eliminate water through the leaves, a process called transpiration. Certain conifers are well adapted to such conditions. For example, on the rocky coast of central California are small forests of Monterey cypresses. Their trunks and branches are twisted by the wind. Their roots are exposed by soil erosion. Their needles are hit by flying salt spray from the ocean. And yet these hardy trees cling to life and continue to grow.

Various soil properties influence plants, including the nature and availability of nutrients, the temperature, the amount of moisture and the air content. For example, much of the coastal plain of the southeastern United States has a sandy soil that is low in nutrients and does not hold water very well. Broadleaf trees do not do well in such soil, but certain species of pines are abundant.

If environmental conditions change, so will the plants that grow in an area. This has happened throughout the

CHANGES IN A FOREST

A power company cuts a broad swath through a forest and erects tall towers to carry power lines. In the process all the plants are removed from the strip of land, which may be 50 feet (15 meters) wide and several miles long. The ground is bare—but not for long. Soon, grasses and wildflowers cover the strip. They are followed by blackberry, currant and other shrubs. In time, willow trees and alders develop, crowding out some of the shrubs and grasses. Later, the willows and alders will be crowded out by maples and oaks, or by hemlocks and other conifers.

Such a series of orderly changes from one kind of community to another is called ecological succession. Eventually, a stable community is formed. New species are not likely to be introduced.

Unless a sudden or violent change occurs, the community remains in a state of balance. This final stage of succession is called a climax community.

Most forests are climax communities. Human activities often interfere with ecological succession. The power company destroyed part of a climax community when it cut its path through the forest. Later, after the towers were constructed, company workers periodically returned to the land. They cut down trees that started to grow near the towers. Thus they prevented the natural succession from one type of ecological community to another.

Earth's history, and it will continue to occur in the future. At the present time, as the climate becomes milder in parts of the Northern Hemisphere, the coniferous forests are slowly moving northward. They are being replaced by deciduous trees, which are better adapted to the warmer temperatures.

There are four major types of forests: coniferous, temperate deciduous, tropical rain and tropical deciduous.

Coniferous Forests

Vast forests of conifers extend across the higher latitudes of the Northern Hemisphere. The largest coniferous forests are in the Soviet Union. Canada is in second place. Third is the United States, where coniferous forests are common in the Cascade, Rocky and Appalachian mountains. Coniferous forests are also found in parts of Brazil, Chile, Southeast Asia, the Philippines and New Zealand.

The climate is generally cold in the northern coniferous forests. Summers are short; winters are long and very cold. Precipitation, including snow, averages from 15 to 30 inches (38–76 centimeters) a year. The growing season—the frost-free period during which leaves are produced and stems lengthen—may be only three or four months long. Thus trees in this environment grow more slowly than do trees in warmer climates with longer growing seasons.

Spruce and fir predominate in many coniferous forests. Pine, hemlock, larch and cedar also are common. The needlelike leaves have a waxy coating that protects against cold and reduces the loss of water to air.

Temperate Deciduous Forests

In more temperate regions, forests are composed mainly of deciduous, or broadleaf, trees that shed their leaves annually. These forests are found principally in the British Isles, central Europe, eastern Asia and the eastern United States. The soil is rich, filled with nutrients and decayed organic matter. Much of the best farmland in places such as western Europe and the United States was once covered by deciduous forests.

The climate is generally moderate. It is characterized by warm summers and cold winters. Precipitation averages from 30 to 60 inches (76–152 centimeters) a year. This moisture is usually distributed rather evenly throughout the year. The growing season usually lasts from 90 to 200 days.

Oak, maple and hickory are common in U.S. forests. Other trees found in temperate deciduous forests include chestnut, elm, basswood, tulip tree, beech and birch.

Tropical Rain Forests

These forests grow in warm equatorial regions that receive a lot of rain. They are found in Central and South America, India, Southeast Asia, the Philippines, northeastern Australia and the Congo River basin in Africa.

It is warm all year long in tropical rain forests, with very little temperature change from month to month. Even in the coolest months, temperatures remain above 64° F (18° C). The forests usually receive from 70 to 200 inches (178–508 centimeters) of rain annually. The rain is normally distributed evenly throughout the year.

Usually, the soil is not very fertile. Almost all of the forest's nutrients are part of the living vegetation. When a plant or

Tropical rain forests are homes for thousands of plant and animal species. Here, a red-eyed tree frog sits atop a perch in the Costa Rican rain forest.

animal dies, it is quickly broken down by bacteria and other decomposing organisms, and its nutrients are soon absorbed by nearby trees.

The dominant plants are broadleaf trees. They remain evergreen because the growing season is year-long.

Tropical Deciduous or Seasonal Forests

Sometimes called dry forests, these occur in parts of Central and South America, Southeast Asia, Indonesia and south and west Africa.

Temperatures are similar to those in tropical rain forests. From 30 to 100 inches (76–250 centimeters) of rain fall

FOSSIL FORESTS

Vast swamps covered much of Pennsylvania 100 million years ago. The dominant plants in the swamps were tree ferns that grew 60 feet (18 meters) or more in height. The ferns formed dense forests that were home to many other plants and animals. As the ferns and other organisms died, they sank into the swamp and began to decay. Over many thousands of years, a thick layer of partially decomposed organic matter gradually formed.

Later the area changed. The swamps dried out. The land sank and was flooded. Tons of sediments were deposited on top. The weight of all this material exerted great pressure on the remains of the tree ferns and other organisms. Under the pressure, the organic matter gradually turned into coal.

Because it formed from decayed organisms that were preserved in the Earth's crust, coal is called a fossil fuel. Oil and natural gas are other types of fossil fuels.

annually. These forests have alternating dry and wet seasons. The trees generally shed their leaves at the beginning of the dry season. Teak was a common tree in such forests that once covered large areas of India, Myanmar and Thailand.

Other Types of Forests

Within each of the major types of forests, there are many variations. At the southern edge of a northern coniferous forest, where it merges with a deciduous forest, mixed forests are common. Mingled among the deciduous maples and oaks are stands of conifers. Similar mixed forests are also seen at higher altitudes in places such as the Appalachian and Great Smoky mountains.

Lower elevations in the southeastern United States—from Florida northward to New Jersey and as far west as Texas—are home to forests of southern pines. These are mostly small or medium-sized trees. In northern areas, pitch pine is the dominant species. Further south, loblolly pine, slash pine and longleaf pine are more abundant.

In the Mediterranean Sea area and parts of California where winters are mild and wet, broad schlerophyll (hard-leaved) forests are typical. In California, eucalyptus trees and certain species of evergreen oaks commonly called live oaks are common in such forests.

On mountain slopes in tropical lands, where the climate is comparatively cool and dry, montane forests grow. They are composed mainly of broadleaf evergreen trees. They resemble tropical rain forests, but they have fewer species, especially at the higher elevations.

Mangrove swamp forests are found in many tropical and subtropical areas around the globe. These forests grow in tidal areas where fresh river water mixes with salty water. The mangroves have massive root systems that help anchor the trees in the mud. In addition, stiltlike roots grow out from the trunk and drop into the swamp, providing additional support for the tree.

Throughout Asia, from sea level to mountain slopes thousands of feet high, forests of bamboo flourish. In Japan alone, there are 662 kinds of bamboo. But bamboo isn't a tree. It's a gigantic grass. Like other grasses, it grows in thick clumps. But like trees it forms woody stems and often grows to great heights.

3

THE FOREST AS AN ECOSYSTEM

Forests are not just masses of trees. They are ecosystems. An ecosystem consists of all the organisms in an area, plus their interactions with one another and with their nonliving surroundings. The organisms include green plants—not only trees but also shrubs, vines, mosses, ferns and grasses. An ecosystem contains animals, too—from tiny insects and worms to large mammals such as jaguars and gorillas. Also present are fungi, such as mushrooms, and one-celled bacteria. The nonliving parts of an ecosystem include sunlight, wind, air, water, rocks and soil.

Trees are the largest organisms in a forest ecosystem. They have the greatest effect on the ecosystem. Without the trees, many other organisms that live in the forest could not survive. Nor could trees survive without many of their neighbors. Fig trees are a good example. These trees are found in most of the world's tropical rain forests. Their juicy fruits are a major source of food for many animals in the forests. According to one estimate, for three months of every year, figs are the main food source for about 75% of all the mammals and birds in the Amazon rain forest. Yet the trees would not form fruits and seeds without tiny insects called agaonid wasps. There are over 900 species of fig trees in the world. Each depends on its own kind of agaonid wasp for pollination. Without pollination, fruits and seeds would not

Opposite page:
The forest floor is just one of the layers in the forest's complex ecosystem. Organisms as small as bacteria and as large as elephants depend on food from the forest floor for survival.

23

Every organism has certain adaptations that enable it to survive and prosper in its environment. Sometimes these adaptations seem quite extraordinary. Consider, for example, certain species of fig trees. They are stranglers.

A strangler fig begins life when a seed—perhaps dropped by a bird or a bat—begins to germinate, or sprout, on the branch of a tall tree in the rain forest. As the tiny fig plant grows, it sends roots down the trunk of the host tree. These aerial roots grow longer and longer until they reach the forest floor. The roots creep beneath the debris on the forest floor and into the soil.

As the fig tree grows, its leaves crowd out the leaves of the host tree. Its roots grow thicker and thicker, gradually squeezing the host tree to death. Eventually the fig's aerial roots fuse and completely enclose the trunk of the host tree. Over time, the host's trunk rots. The fig, now a massive tree with a hollow core, stands as one of the giants of the tropical rain forest. Its fruits are a vital source of food for numerous animals. Parrots, hornbills, bulbuls, gibbons, flying foxes, bats and many other creatures come to feed. Many other animals, including geckos, frogs and paper wasps, make their home in the hollow trunk.

form. Without seeds, the trees would be unable to reproduce. Without new trees, the species would become extinct. There would be no more fig trees—and no more figs for spider monkeys, toucans and other animals to eat.

Layers of the Forest

Each forest is unique, with its own unique set of species. Yet there are similarities among the world's forests. They have certain features in common. Among these is structure. All forests are made up of horizontal layers.

The highest layer in a forest is formed by the tops of the tallest trees. The lowest layer is the ground. Each layer is a habitat, or place where organisms live. What is interesting is that each layer contains its own unique mix of plants and animals. Even organisms that are very similar may occupy different layers. A study of birds conducted in New York State forests found that different kinds of warblers live in the forests. One kind lives in the highest treetops. Another kind lives in smaller trees. Still other kinds live in shrubs or near the ground. This is actually very beneficial to the warblers. By living in different parts of the forest, the birds do not compete with one another.

The layer formed by the tops of the tallest trees is called the canopy. This layer receives the greatest amount of sunlight, so it is the layer where most of the forest's photosynthesis takes place. In some forests, the canopy is a dense, continuous layer many feet thick. Little sunlight penetrates to lower layers. This restricts the growth of shorter plants. In other forests, the treetops that form the canopy are widely spaced. Sunlight reaches shrubs, grasses and other plants at lower levels, enabling them to prosper.

Some forest animals avoid higher parts of the canopy because of the intense sunlight and often harsh weather conditions. Numerous leaf-eating insect species are among the exceptions. Aphids, leaf miners and leaf hoppers are among the insects that are plentiful in the canopy. Their presence helps attract insect-eating birds, as well as spiders and insects that eat insects. Squirrels scramble through the canopy, gathering seeds and nuts. Some of the squirrels have winglike membranes that allow them to glide from branch to branch. Eagles, crows and hawks perch high in the trees, watching for prey.

Immediately below the canopy is the understory. This layer consists of the tops of shorter trees. Some of these trees, unable to compete with the taller trees, eventually die. Others continue growing until they become dominant trees and form part of the canopy.

Animal life is generally abundant in the understory, particularly if plants are lush. Many birds nest here. Insects are plentiful. Jumping spiders, which have well-developed eyes and excellent vision, hunt the insects. In Borneo, orangutans and gibbons use their long, powerful arms to swing from branch to branch and from tree to tree. They often move high into the canopy but seldom set foot to the ground. Along the Congo River in Africa, gorillas spend the daylight hours feeding on the ground, then move into the trees at night. They weave branches and vines together to form platforms on which to sleep.

In many forests, especially rain forests, epiphytes are common in the lower part of the canopy and in the understory. Orchids are examples of tropical epiphytes. Epiphytes are plants that grow upon other plants. They generally grow on the tree trunks or in the notch of a branch. They do not obtain nourishment from the supporting host plant. Rather, they depend on their own roots. The roots help to hold the epiphyte to the object on which it grows. In addition, the roots are exposed to the air, and they are able to absorb water from the atmosphere. The roots can also absorb nutrients from debris that collects around them. Sometimes the roots even contain chlorophyll and are able to manufacture food. Communities of insects, centipedes and even small frogs are often present in the tangle of epiphytic leaves and roots.

If the canopy allows quite a bit of light to penetrate to lower levels, there may be a shrub layer. Shrubs are woody plants with several stems growing out of the ground. An even lower layer of herbs—plants without woody stems—may also

THE LIVING DEAD

During a vicious storm, lightning hits a tall tree in the forest, splitting its trunk. The upper part of the tree crashes to the forest floor. The lower part, jagged and branchless, remains erect.

Before long, woodpeckers drill holes in the rough piece, or snag, left standing. Squirrels store food supplies in some of the holes. Mushrooms and mosses sprout on the fallen branches. A mouse builds a nest in a protected tangle of branches. Centipedes and green snakes burrow beneath the bark. Ants and beetles tunnel into the rotting wood. A salamander follows, to lay its eggs in the wood. Bacteria and fungi break down the wood, releasing its nutrients to the soil.

The tree is dead, but it is filled with life. And its gradual decomposition will give life to new trees, in a continuing cycle that maintains the richness of the forest ecosystem.

be present. It consists of grasses, wildflowers, ferns and mosses. If these plants are plentiful, songbirds will flit about, feeding on berries and seeds. Small mammals such as chipmunks and mice will also be common.

The forest floor is covered with litter that falls from the upper layers: leaves, branches, dead animals and so on. Lizards and snakes hunt for mice and other small mammals. Spiders and scorpions feed on insects. Millipedes lay eggs under the bark of fallen trunks. Beetles dig tunnels in wood. Bacteria and fungi help decompose the dead organic matter. Earthworms crawl between the surface and underground passageways.

Many large animals live on the forest floor. Anteaters and tapirs root for insects. Reindeer feed on mosses and grasses. Elephants use their trunks to strip leaves and branches off trees. At night, tigers hunt, attacking large prey in terrifying bursts of speed.

The soil is the lowest layer of the forest. Held in place by massive root systems, the soil is home to insects, worms and many other small organisms. These organisms bring bits of decaying organic matter into the soil from the surface, helping to enrich the soil. Their burrows allow air and water to easily enter the soil.

The Greatest Show on Earth

Tropical rain forests are Earth's richest ecosystems. They teem with life. According to the U.S. National Academy of Sciences, a typical patch of rain forest covering 4 square miles (10.4 square kilometers) contains 750 species of trees, 750 species of other plants, 125 species of mammals, 400 species of birds, 100 species of reptiles and 60 species of amphibians.

The largest tropical rain forest is the rain forest in the Amazon River basin of South America. It truly deserves to be called the greatest show on Earth! This rain forest supports more kinds of plants and animals than any other ecosystem on our planet. Some 40,000 species of plants have been identified in the Amazon rain forest. The variety of plants does not equal the incredible diversity displayed by the

THE FOREST COMMUNITY

Canopy

Trees

Understory

Birds

Decay

Shrub layer

Water fowl

Soil

Insects

Herb layer

Ferns

Flowers

Animals

Forest floor

Microbes

Worms

Grasses

Water plants

Water life

millions of animal species, however—many of which have not yet been "discovered" and studied by scientists.

The Amazon River is formed by streams that begin in the Andes Mountains of Peru. It flows eastward across Brazil to empty into the Atlantic Ocean. The world's second longest river after the Nile, the Amazon is approximately 4,000 miles (6,437 kilometers) in length. It is fed by more than 1,000 tributaries and carries nearly 20% of all the water discharged into the Earth's oceans. Every hour, the Amazon empties an average of 170 billion gallons (643 billion liters) of water into the Atlantic. That's more than 30 gallons (113 liters) of water per hour for each human being on Earth.

The majority of the Amazon basin—the land drained by the Amazon River and its tributaries—is in Brazil. The basin also extends into eight other countries: French Guiana, Suriname, Guyana, Venezuela, Colombia, Ecuador, Peru and Bolivia. Altogether, the river and forest system covers 2.7 million square miles (7 million square kilometers), an area more than 10 times as large as Texas, 17 times as large as California or 525 times as large as Connecticut.

In the virgin forest—those areas that have not suffered massive cutting by human beings—the canopy is very dense throughout the year. From the air, it appears to form a vast green blanket. Only where a meandering river cuts through the forest is there a break in the green.

Here and there an exceptionally tall tree towers above the top of the canopy. These trees are called emergents. They may be 200 feet (60 meters) tall. They tend to have small leaves. The leaves at the top of the canopy are also small. Lower in the forest, where there is less light, the plants have large, spearlike leaves. These big leaves are often thick, to store moisture, and covered with a layer of shiny wax, to reduce water loss through transpiration.

The main canopy is formed by trees 100 to 165 feet (30 to 50 meters) tall. Crowding up from underneath are slightly smaller trees. All the trees are broadleaf evergreens. Their foliage prevents almost all light from penetrating to the forest floor. As a result, the floor is in deep shade. Relatively few shrubs and herbs grow there. In many spots the floor is bare except for a thin litter of leaves. Thick masses of tree roots are common, however, snaking along the ground, branching and rebranching. Delicate root tips push into litter to absorb the nutrients released by bacteria and other decomposers. Debris does not last long on the forest floor, and nutrients move rapidly back into the growing plants. The rain forest recycles nutrients so efficiently that almost no decaying matter enters the rivers.

The rain forest trees have surprisingly shallow roots. This is beneficial in collecting water and nutrients, but it makes the tree unstable. In some species, added support for the trunk and crown are provided by giant buttresses growing outward from the trunk. Other trees produce roots that grow downward from the trunk or branches—rather like crutches "growing" downward from the armpits of a person with a broken leg. In addition to providing support, the auxiliary roots help the tree compete for the nutrients and water deep in the ground below.

At all levels of the forest are mosses, ferns, vines and epiphytes. Some vines have such thick stems and twine so densely around a tree that they can hold the tree upright after it has been cut by a chainsaw. These vines may also be parasites. Parasites are organisms that obtain food from another organism, called the host; in the process, the host is harmed. The roots of parasitic vines grow into the tree itself and absorb food and moisture stored by the tree.

Orchids are common epiphytes in the Amazon forest. Up to 50 species of orchids have been found on a single tree. Another interesting group of Amazonian epiphytes are the bromeliads. Relatives of the pineapple, they have long branching leaves that overlap tightly at their bases. This forms a container that catches rain and debris. Large bromeliads may hold a gallon (4 liters) or more of water. These water tanks are like miniature ponds, providing homes for frogs, snails and aquatic insects. They are visited by snakes, birds and other thirsty, hungry creatures. They are also "visited" by the trees on which the bromeliads grow; trees often send out feeder roots into the organic debris accumulated by epiphytes growing on their trunks and branches.

Animals of the Amazon forest are adapted to life in different layers. Some spend their entire lives in the canopy, never setting foot on the ground. One such creature is the three-toed sloth. It spends most of its time hanging upside down from a branch. At night, it moves slowly in search of tasty leaves and buds. The sloth has strong claws to provide a secure grip. Other canopy dwellers have long, flexible tails that function as a fifth leg. The grip of a spider monkey's tail is so strong that it can support all the animal's body weight. Capuchin monkeys, which travel in long, single-file lines, reportedly use their tails to form living bridges over which the rest of the group pass from tree to tree.

Among the forest's fiercest predators is the harpy eagle. Its tough, clawed feet are as large as a man's hands, and powerful enough to tear monkeys and sloths out of the canopy. Another powerful predator is the jaguar—the biggest wildcat in the Americas. Though it weighs up to 300 pounds (136 kilograms), it is a good climber and often feeds on birds. It is a good swimmer, too, and easily catches turtles and fish.

Many Amazonian animals are extremely colorful. Sometimes, the color serves as a warning. The toucan has a massive bill colored in shades of red, blue and green—which may be attractive to mates but may frighten would-be predators. Dendrobatid frogs have strikingly bright colors. One is a vivid red. Another is black with brilliant yellow stripes. All dendrobatids secrete very strong poisons through their skins. The poison is so effective against birds and other small animals that local Indians collect the frogs and extract the poison, which they use on the tips of arrows.

The largest animal populations are found on the forest floor. They include huge columns of army ants marching in search of small animals on which to feed. As many as 20 million ants may form one of these swarms. As the swarm advances, some insects in its path manage to escape. The escape may be brief, however, for many birds follow the ants, grabbing the hopping, flying insects for their dinners.

Changing with the Seasons

One of nature's most glorious sights is an autumn forest in New England. The hills are covered by a blaze of reds, oranges and yellows as the leaves of oaks, maples and other deciduous trees turn color. After the colorful autumn display, the leaves die and fall from the branches. As many as 10 million leaves may fall from the trees in one acre (0.4 hectare) of forest. Throughout the winter, the branches are bare. Then, as warm weather and longer days return to New England, buds burst open, producing bright green leaves.

The seasonal changes of the trees result from the seasonal changes in climate. Unlike the Amazon rain forest, the temperate deciduous forests of New England must survive extremes. In summer, temperatures may be higher than those in the Amazon. In winter, icy winds whip through the forest and the ground is covered with snow. Precipitation is not as great as in the tropics. And while it falls rather regularly throughout the year, much of the winter supply of water is locked up in snow and frost, unavailable for immediate use by plants.

The New England forest does not have anywhere near as many species as the Amazon. Its variety is a result of the changing seasons, as each species adapts in unique ways to survive through the year.

The dominant trees are oak, maple, hickory and walnut. Like the Amazonian trees, they are broadleaf trees. However, they are deciduous, dropping their leaves in autumn. This stops transpiration, or water loss, from leaves, enabling the trees to preserve water stored in the cells of their roots, trunk and branches. Because the leaves are gone, no photosynthesis occurs. The trees do not grow during the winter months but are dormant. They use only minimal amounts of stored water and food to produce the energy needed to remain alive.

Another difference in the trees of the two ecosystems is found in the root systems. The oak and most other northern deciduous trees have taproot systems. There is one large central root, the taproot, that grows straight down. Numerous smaller roots branch from the taproot, then branch over

THE ROOT SYSTEM

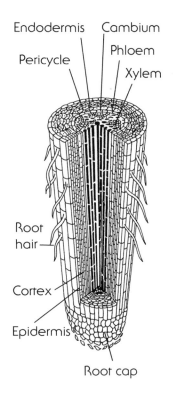

Endodermis Cambium

Pericycle

Phloem

Xylem

Root hair

Cortex

Epidermis

Root cap

and over again to form a fibrous horizontal network. The taproot provides firm anchorage in the soil, protecting the tree against windstorms. It also enables the tree to reach nutrients and water located deep in the ground. The other roots help stabilize the tree and absorb materials from the surface layer of soil.

When the calendar year begins in January, New England forests are all buried in snow. Tree branches are bare and there are no signs of plant growth in the forest. But a woodpecker can be heard, drilling through the bark of trees in search of insects. A look at the snow reveals footprints of deer and several other mammals. These animals have adaptations that enable them to remain active during the harsh weather. In autumn, deer grow a winter coat of hollow hairs that traps warm air against the body. The snowshoe hare loses its brown summer fur and changes to a thicker white coat, which not only provides warmth but also helps to make the hare "invisible" to hungry foxes.

Other animals adapt to winter by avoiding it. Many of the birds that fill the spring and summer forest with song fly south in autumn, to spend the winter in warmer places. Some insects spin insulating cocoons around themselves; others die after laying eggs that can survive until spring. Bears curl up in a den and go to sleep, occasionally awakening and going outside on warm, sunny days. Woodchucks, chipmunks, jumping mice and some bats crawl into burrows or caves and hibernate. During hibernation, an animal's breathing, heartbeat and other body processes slow down. The woodchuck, for example, has a heart beat of about 80 times per minute when it is active during the summer. During hibernation, the heart beats only four or five times a minute. Like the oak trees, the hibernating animals live off food stored in certain body cells.

In spring, as days become longer and temperatures rise, the first signs of plant life are seen on the ground. Tiny flowers called snowdrops push through the snow and decaying piles of leaves. As the snow melts, the forest floor becomes covered with violets, trilliums, and other small herbs. Shrubs burst

A NEW MONKEY

The identification of a new species of ant or flea may not impress ordinary people. Every so often, however, our list of known species increases because of a truly exciting discovery. This was the case in 1990, when two Brazilian scientists reported the discovery of a previously unknown species of monkey. The species is a type of lion tamarin and one of the most brilliantly colored mammals. Its body is covered with a rich golden fur. It has a black face, black forearms and a black tail.

The animal was discovered in Brazil's Atlantic forest, a rain forest far to the south of the Amazon. Several hundred years ago, this forest was immense. It edged the coast for some 2,000 miles (3,200 kilometers). But over the centuries the forest has been cut down. Sugarcane and coffee plantations, highways and dams, cities and factories have replaced it. Today, less than 5% of the Atlantic forest remains. Each year, the forest continues to shrink, as farmers and developers cut down its trees. Each year, the threat of extinction increases for the lion tamarin and other animals found nowhere else on Earth.

into bloom. The herbs and shrubs flower and grow while sunlight still reaches them. Soon, buds on the small trees burst open and give rise to a new crop of leaves that partially shades the ground. Then medium-sized trees and finally the tall oaks and hickories open their leaves.

By the beginning of summer, the canopy is dense. Below it, there are deep shadows. Temperatures and humidity are high, creating an environment attractive to mushrooms, which become numerous on the forest floor, where they obtain nourishment from last year's leaves and other decaying plant matter. Earthworms and other small creatures also help break down the plant matter. Their activity adds large amounts of nutrients to the soil, making the soil thick and rich.

During a summer day, it is quiet in the forest. Most of the mammals and many of the birds rest. They are active at night, when temperatures are cooler. Opossums and porcupines forage among the litter on the forest floor. Foxes, skunks and deer wander into nearby fields in their search for food.

Activity picks up as autumn approaches. Trees produce nuts that contain the seeds for new trees. Squirrels gather some of the nuts and store them as food for the winter. Beavers pile up tree branches and bark near their lodges. And on the trees, the green leaves begin to change color.

4

WHY PEOPLE
NEED FORESTS

For thousands of people, forests are home. The Ituri rain forest of the Congo River basin in northeastern Zaire is home to the Mbuti. Calling themselves "children of the forest," the Mbuti depend on the forest for all the essentials of life. Their food consists of fruits, nuts, mushrooms and roots gathered in the forest, supplemented by game. The animals are shot with arrows tipped with poison or caught in nets made of vines. The Mbuti live in huts built with saplings, then covered with large leaves. They wear loincloths made from tree bark that has been pounded until it is thin and soft.

Like the Mbuti, people everywhere depend on forests to fill important daily needs. The paper on which these words are printed was once part of a forest. It was part of a tree, perhaps one that was hundreds of feet tall and centuries old. Many other products that people take for granted were also part of forests: furniture, houses, cardboard boxes, rubber, foods and spices, oils, medicines and so on.

Forests are much more than sources of food and material goods, however, They affect the composition of the atmosphere. They regulate and moderate climate. They conserve soil and water. They create habitats for millions of species.

Opposite page: Some humans around the globe have successfully inhabited forests without destroying them. Others have cleared trees for large housing developments and industrial sites that disrupted a natural and delicate balance and caused irreparable habitat loss for countless living species.

Environmental Cycles

Within the ecosystem, certain substances are constantly being recycled. Two of the most important of these are oxygen and carbon. Trees play a central role in these cycles.

Trees and other green plants contain the green pigment chlorophyll in their leaf cells. This enables the plants to make their own food. The process is called photosynthesis—a term derived from Greek words meaning "putting together with light." In addition to chlorophyll, photosynthesis requires light energy, water and carbon dioxide. The sun is the source of trees' light energy. Water enters trees through the roots. Carbon dioxide, a component of air, enters through tiny openings in the leaves called stomata.

The light energy is absorbed by the chlorophyll and used to break apart the water molecules into hydrogen and oxygen. The oxygen is released into the atmosphere. The hydrogen from the water molecules combines with the carbon dioxide to form the simplest carbohydrate, the sugar glucose. Then in a series of additional reactions, the glucose (often in combination with other elements) serves as building blocks for additional compounds needed by the plants: other carbohydrates, proteins, fats and vitamins. These compounds, all containing carbon, are called organic compounds.

Green plants convert huge amounts of carbon dioxide into sugar and other organic compounds. It has been estimated that plants consume 500 billion tons of carbon dioxide every year, converting it into organic matter and oxygen. Trees—the largest plants—absorb the most carbon dioxide and store the greatest amount of carbon, most of it in their woody tissues. A forest of trees stores millions of times more carbon than a field of corn. Indeed, forests are the major stockpiles of carbon. The trees of the rain forest of the Amazon River basin store at least 75 billion tons of carbon!

Eventually, most of the carbon stored in trees is returned to the atmosphere. Some is returned as cells in the trees break down carbon compounds for energy. This process, called respiration, is in some ways the reverse of photosynthesis. The carbon compounds are broken down into glucose. The

STRUCTURE OF A TYPICAL LEAF

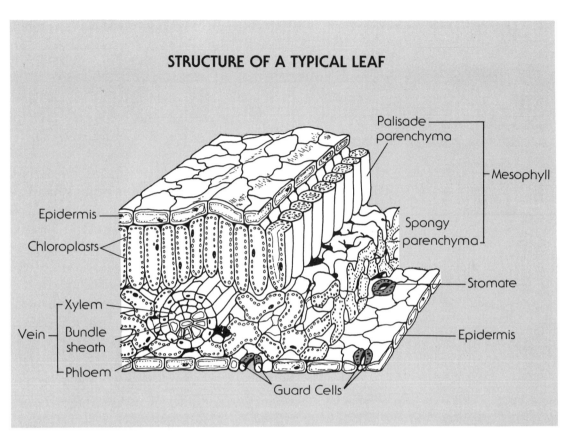

Palisade parenchyma

Mesophyll

Epidermis

Chloroplasts

Spongy parenchyma

Stomate

Xylem

Vein — Bundle sheath

Phloem

Epidermis

Guard Cells

STOMATE CLOSED AND OPEN

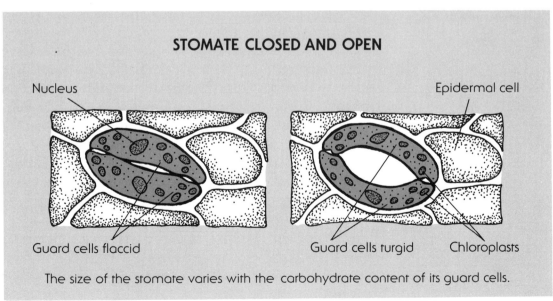

Nucleus

Epidermal cell

Guard cells flaccid

Guard cells turgid

Chloroplasts

The size of the stomate varies with the carbohydrate content of its guard cells.

glucose combines with oxygen from the atmosphere. Water and carbon dioxide are formed and diffuse out into the environment. Energy released during the process is used by the cells for growth and repair.

Animals cannot make their own food. They depend, directly or indirectly, on green plants for food—and for oxygen. When a deer eats the leaves of a tree, the organic compounds are digested. Some are used to build and maintain body cells. Others are broken down and burned for energy, in the same respiration process found in plants. The deer obtains the needed oxygen from the atmosphere. If green plants did not make food and emit oxygen, deer and all other animals would be unable to exist.

When the deer is killed and eaten by a pack of wolves, the same processes of digestion and respiration occur. In this manner, the carbon is transferred from one organism to another. And much of it is exhaled back into the atmosphere as carbon dioxide.

When plants and animals die, bacteria and fungi feed on the remains. They, too, digest the carbon compounds, obtaining the energy they need to survive and in the process giving off carbon dioxide.

The carbon cycle is not in perfect balance. Because of their long life spans, trees store carbon for many centuries. Also, not all plant and animal tissues are broken down. Some are trapped and transformed into coal and other fossil fuels. Only when people burn these substances is the carbon released back into the atmosphere. This may be long after the carbon was stored in the organisms. For instance, the coal we burn was formed from giant plants that lived many millions of years ago.

If large amounts of the carbon that is locked up in trees and fossil fuels are released—through deforestation and excessive burning of fuels—then the level of carbon dioxide in the atmosphere increases. This is happening today. Carbon dioxide is being added to the atmosphere faster than it can be removed by the Earth's green plants. This is causing the temperature of the atmosphere to rise, a phenomenon that is discussed in Chapter 6.

Modifying Climate

Trees also play an important role in the water cycle: the movement of water from one part of the environment to another. Trees absorb enormous amounts of water through their roots. They take in much more than they use for growth. Most of the water absorbed by trees is transpired, or eliminated, through the tiny stomata in the leaves. Each leaf has hundreds of thousands of stomata. Thus a birch tree, with some 200,000 leaves, may transpire as much as 900 gallons (3,400 liters) of water on a warm summer day.

The large amount of water given off by all the leaves in a forest can strongly influence local climate. It can increase the humidity and rainfall of an area. When large forest areas are cut down, less rain falls on those areas. In central Panama, almost all the rain forests have been cleared and replaced by cattle ranches. Records show that annual rainfall in central Panama decreased by 17 inches (43 centimeters) between 1925 and 1985.

By shading the ground from direct sunlight, trees affect air temperatures. Ordinarily, air temperatures within forests are several degrees cooler than temperatures in neighboring nonforested areas. Trees also act as windbreaks. They lessen the force of the wind and even change its direction of movement. This can be extremely valuable to farmers. In flat regions such as the Great Plains of North America, trees planted as windbreaks prevent snow—the main source of moisture for spring crops—from blowing off fields. Windbreaks also protect against excessive transpiration caused by winds. One study found that planting trees and hedges around small grain fields can increase crop yields by 20% because the trees and hedges protect the fields from the drying effects of winds.

Many people plant trees around their homes to take advantage of the trees' moderating effects. Studies have shown that the proper placement of trees and shrubs can lower a home's need for heating and cooling by 25% or more. Dense evergreen trees and shrubs create shade and block winds. They also create "dead" air spaces between the plants and the house, which helps insulate the home. Deciduous trees provide shade during hot summer months but allow the sun's energy to reach and warm the house during winter months.

Soil and Water

The roots of a single grass plant, if laid end to end, may total 400 miles (644 kilometers) in length. Imagine then, the total length of all the roots of a giant tree! No one has ever measured the root system of a tree. The task is probably impossible. One difficulty is that there are millions of tiny root tips. Spreading outward from each root tip are thousands of microscopic root hairs.

The root tips and hairs attach so tightly to grains of soil that they cannot be removed without being broken. This helps to anchor the tree. It also helps to hold the soil, preventing the soil from being washed away by falling rain or melting snow. This conserves the soil. It also prevents the soil

RELATIVE SIZES OF EVERGREEN TREES

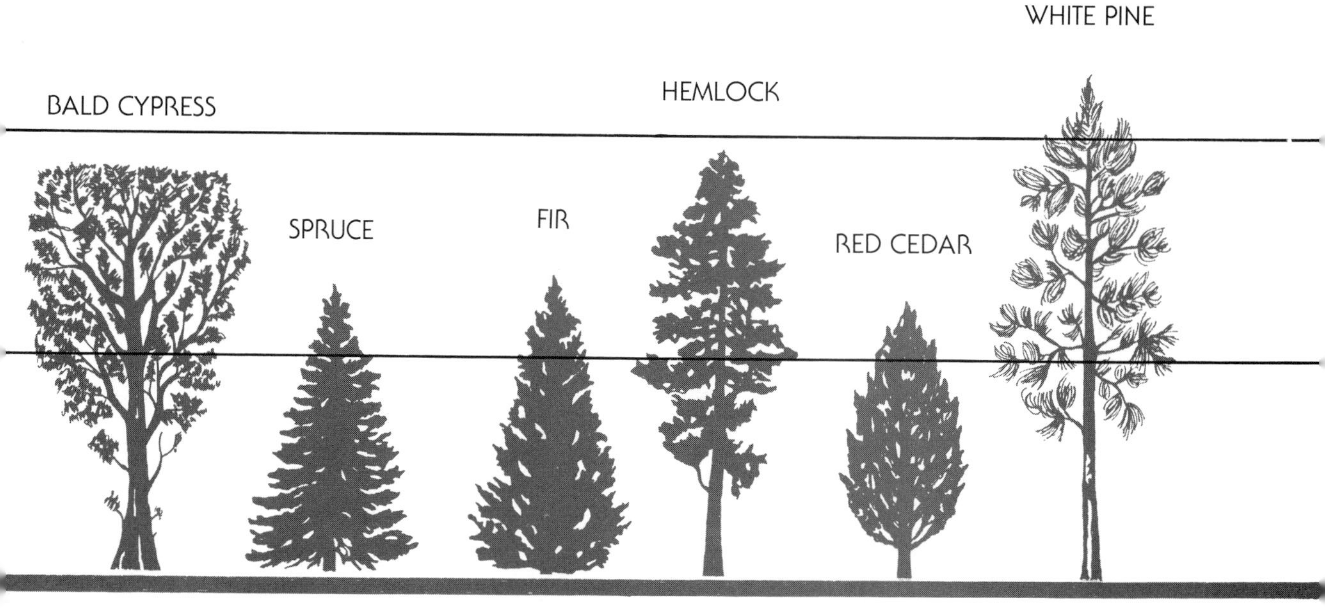

WHITE PINE

HEMLOCK

BALD CYPRESS

SPRUCE

FIR

RED CEDAR

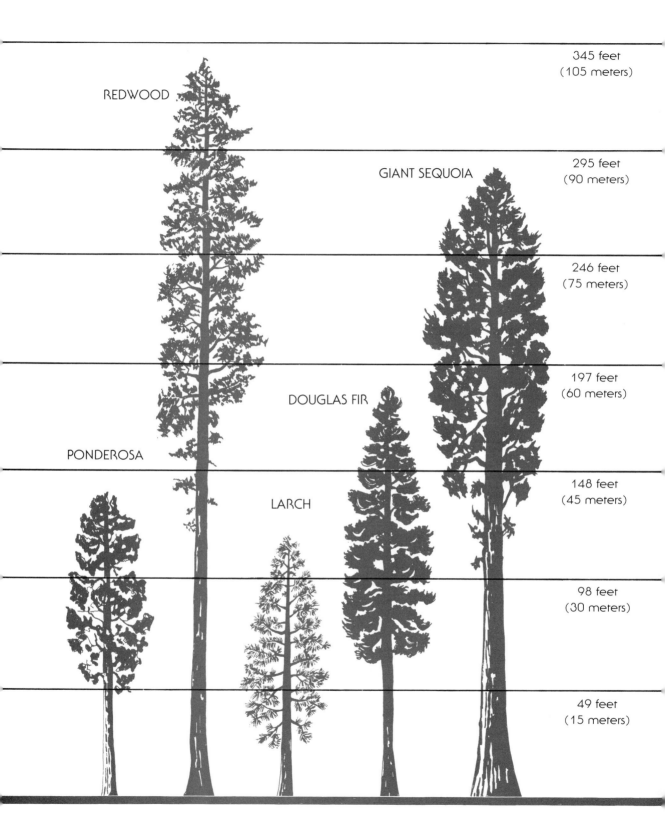

REDWOOD

GIANT SEQUOIA

345 feet
(105 meters)

295 feet
(90 meters)

246 feet
(75 meters)

DOUGLAS FIR

197 feet
(60 meters)

PONDEROSA

LARCH

148 feet
(45 meters)

98 feet
(30 meters)

49 feet
(15 meters)

from being carried into streams and lakes, where it can cause a form of pollution called siltation. Siltation is harmful to many organisms. For example, in mountain streams, even small amounts of siltation can prevent the reproduction of certain aquatic insects that are eaten by trout. Without the insects, the trout cannot survive.

Forests also help form soil. As tree roots push deep into the ground, they break the rocky subsoil into ever smaller pieces. Eventually, the rocky pieces are broken down into sand and other mineral particles. As the trees die and are decomposed, they also enrich the soil with organic matter.

Forests play important roles in the conservation of water. As rain falls on a forest, its force is broken by the canopy of treetops. Instead of pouring down on the soil, the water slowly drips off branches and dribbles down trunks. This protects against erosion by providing time for the water to seep into the soil.

In high mountain forests, where deep layers of soil build up during winter months, the trees shade the snow from the sun and protect it from drying winds. Thus the snow melts slowly during the spring and summer months, allowing much of the moisture to seep into the ground, where it can be absorbed by the trees.

Land covered with trees can absorb much more water than land without trees. Roots and burrowing animals have opened up countless spaces, making the soil resemble a giant sponge. This is important in providing the plants with a steady supply of moisture. It also is important in conserving water for other uses.

The land from which water drains into a lake or stream is called a watershed. When the land is forested, water seeps into the lake or stream at a comparatively constant pace. This protects against destructive and wasteful floods. It also provides a steady supply of water with which to irrigate lowland farms and quench the thirsts of millions of people in communities large and small. The residents of New York City, for example, depend on forested watersheds north of the city for much of their drinking water.

THE SECRET OF SILK

More than 4,000 years ago, someone discovered how to produce silk fabric. According to Chinese legend, the inventor was Hsi-ling-chi, the 14-year-old wife of Emperor Huang-ti. Knowledge of the process was kept a closely guarded secret for more than 2,000 years. Long after silk fabric became known in Europe, people there did not know the source of the fabric. Most Europeans believed that silk grew on trees. Others thought it was a fiber taken from the inside of tree bark. Not until A.D. 552 did people in Europe learn the truth: silk is made by a caterpillar.

The caterpillar—also called a silkworm—is the young form of the silkworm moth. In China and several other Asian countries, cultivating silkworms is an important industry. So, too, is growing food for the silkworms, for the creatures are voracious eaters.

A silkworm is very tiny at birth. It is also very hungry. It won't eat just anything. It wants the leaves of mulberry trees. People who raise silkworms also raise mulberry trees. They pick leaves and chop them into small pieces. Every two to three hours, they feed the chopped leaves to the silkworms, which are kept on trays in warm rooms.

In 5 weeks, a silkworm has grown to about 70 times its original size. It is now ready to enter a resting stage. From spe-cial glands in its body, the silkworm exudes fluid silk. This fluid hardens into a thread as it comes in contact with air. The silkworm winds the thread round and round its body, to form a cocoon. If left undisturbed, the silkworm will turn into an adult moth while it is in the cocoon.

But silkworm growers heat the cocoons to kill the insects. Then the people carefully unwind the thread. The thread may be more than 3,000 feet (914 meters) long—an amazing feat for a creature that is less than 3 inches (7.6 centimeters) long.

Most silk is produced by domestically reared silkworms, fed leaves from mulberry trees raised on plantations. A lot of mulberry trees must be grown to meet people's demand for silk. About 25,000 cocoons are needed to make a pound of silk. This translates into 25,000 very hungry silkworms.

In some parts of China and India, forest-dwelling people produce silk from wild tasar silkworms that feed on a variety of wild trees. The trees that can support tasar silkworms also are found in other tropical lands. The U.S. Office of Technology Assessment points out that "this seems to offer significant opportunity for other developing countries to develop industry, employment, income and a raised standard of living for forest-dwelling people while encouraging maintenance of forest ecosystems. . . ."

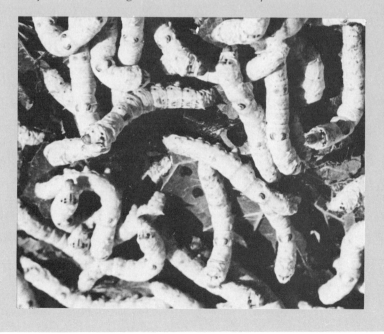

Two studies helped confirm the value of forests in conserving water. In a forested area in Kenya, water measurements were recorded in two adjacent valleys for more than 25 years. When one valley was cleared for a tea plantation, the immediate effect was a fourfold increase in water flow following a rainstorm. In India, the severely eroded Siwalik hills were planted with new forests. As a result, the peak rate of flow from the watershed was reduced 73%, and the total flow was reduced 28%.

Resources for Human Use

Every aspect of people's lives may be affected by products derived from forests. This is a result of the biological richness of the world's forests. Thousands of forest species have proven to be beneficial to us. Trees may head the list, but vines, shrubs and animals also contribute directly to our well-being.

Fuel

Ever since people first discovered fire, wood has been an important fuel for heating and cooking. Today, it is the main source of energy for almost half the world's population. In addition to household use, wood is an important industrial fuel, particularly in tropical regions. Frequently, the wood is made into charcoal. Some countries, such as Brazil, have planted millions of acres of tree plantations to supply fuel wood and charcoal to iron mills and other industries. But these countries also cut virgin rain forests for industrial fuel. In 1988, for example, it was reported that the blast furnaces being constructed in the Brazilian state of Para would begin reducing iron ore to produce pig iron. The process requires a reducing agent such as charcoal. To produce enough charcoal, more than 500,000 acres (202,350 hectares) of forest would have to be cut each year.

Timber and Pulp

Wood is a valued raw material, used in great quantities all over the world. A typical American house may require wood from about 26 125-foot- (38-meter-) tall Douglas firs—for roofing, floors, doors, window frames and so on. Wood is also used in cabinets, shelving and furniture. Baskets, boxes and toys contain wood. Decks and fences are made of wood. So are power and telephone poles, railroad cross ties, docks and piers, commercial buildings and hundreds of other products.

The bulk of the world's paper is made from the cellulose in ground-up wood, or pulp. With the addition of various chemicals, cellulose can also be made into rayon, cellophane and explosives.

Different woods have different characteristics, which makes them suitable for different uses. Fir, pine and spruce are commonly used for house construction. Furniture makers favor maple, mahogany, cherry, oak and teak. White spruce is resilient, quickly returning to its original shape or position after it is bent or stretched; it is often used to make sounding boards of musical instruments. White oak is both strong and long-lasting; it has long been favored for making barrels and buckets, and in building bridges, barns and ships. Walnut is beautifully patterned; it is popular with gun makers. Hickory wood is extremely tough, strong and elastic; it is commonly used for tool handles and archery bows. When burned, hickory has a pleasant scent, and it is used for smoking bacon and hams.

Foods

Forest fruits, nuts, leaves, roots, honey and wild animals are a significant source of food for many of the world's people, particularly in developing countries.

In New England, sugar maple trees are tapped early each spring to obtain sap laden with sugar. The sap is boiled down to produce maple syrup. Between 30 and 40 gallons (113–150 liters) of sap are needed to make one gallon (3.8 liters) of syrup.

Some forest plants are a source of spices and flavorings. Bay leaves come from a shrub or tree common to European forests. Cinnamon is made from the bark of a tree that originated in India and Sri Lanka. Cardamom seeds come from a tree native to East Africa and Madagascar. The bark of the sassafras tree of the eastern United States is the source of an oil used to flavor root beer, candy and baked goods.

Many important crop plants originated in tropical rain forests. Corn is believed to have originated in Peru. Wild relatives of domesticated corn still live in South American forests. They are an important source of genetic material for plant scientists who try to develop improved crop varieties. Similarly, there are wild varieties of cocoa and peanuts in Amazon forests, wild coffee trees in West African forests, wild sugarcane in forests of the South Pacific, and so on.

Medicines

Indians who live in the Amazon rain forest reportedly use at least 1,300 plant species for medicinal purposes. Natives of other tropical areas also use numerous rain forest plants in treatments for a wide range of ailments. Although many of these plants remain to be studied and tested by scientists, others have become the source of medicines used throughout the world. At least one-quarter of the prescription drugs used in the United States were originally derived from or inspired by plants that live in rain forests.

One of the most valuable tropical plants is the rosy periwinkle, which is also called the Madagascar periwinkle. A small herb with pinkish flowers, it contains numerous chemicals found in scarcely any other plants. Some of these chemicals can be used to reduce blood pressure. Others help to lower the concentration of sugar in the blood. But the two most important drugs developed from the rosy periwinkle are vincristine and vinblastine. They are anti-tumor drugs, and they have been extremely valuable in fighting certain types of cancers. Other tropical plants also produce unique anti-cancer compounds. Indeed, 70% of the 3,000 plant species identified by the U.S. National Cancer Institute as having anti-cancer properties are natives of tropical rain forests.

Some of the poisons used by forest natives to stun and kill birds and other prey have become valuable drugs. In South America, the Rayas Indians tip their arrows with curare, a poison obtained from the bark of a vine. Scientists have isolated the chemicals in curare; one, d-tubocurasine, is now widely used to relax the muscles of patients undergoing surgery. The heart medicine strophanthin comes from a West African vine that has long been used as an arrow poison.

Other Products

Some trees, pine in particular, produce a resin that is useful to the trees in walling off wounds. People use resin to make chemicals such as turpentine and rosin. The resin is obtained by tapping pine trees during the growing season, by distilling remains of dead trees or as a by-product of the paper-making process. Another tree, an acacia tree native to regions of Africa and the Middle East, produces a wound substance that is used to make gum arabic, the adhesive commonly used on stamps and envelopes.

Tannin, a yellowish to light-brown substance derived from the bark of various trees, is used in the tanning of animal hides to make leather. The tannin halts decay by forming chemical bonds with the skin tissues.

Wax palms that grow in windy parts of Brazil secrete thick layers of wax from their leaves, to protect against drying. This wax is the hardest of all natural waxes, and it has the highest melting point. The wax is collected by drying the leaves and then beating them to remove the wax. The wax is used in polishes, waterproofing and a variety of other ways.

The outer bark of the cork oak, a tree that grows around the Mediterranean Sea, can be stripped, flattened and treated to form cork. Cork is lightweight, resilient, waterproof, buoyant and able to absorb vibrations. These qualities make it suitable for shoe soles, bottle stoppers, floats and life preservers and sound insulation.

5

GOING, GOING ... GONE

Forests are destroyed by many forces. Some are leveled by natural events, such as violent storms and lightning-sparked fires. Most deforestation, however, is the result of human activities. People use chain saws and axes to clear vast areas. They set fire to forests to create land for farms in primitive "slash and burn" agriculture. They destroy forests indirectly by emitting poisonous pollutants into the atmosphere.

Losses are occurring wherever there are forests—on every continent except Antarctica (which is covered by ice and has no forests), plus on thousands of islands scattered throughout the world's oceans. The most serious losses are occurring in tropical forests. As the 1990s began, Brazil, with the largest tropical forest area, was experiencing the greatest losses: between 12.5 million and 22.5 million acres (5 million and 9 million hectares) annually. India was losing 3.7 million acres (1.5 million hectares) a year. Indonesia was losing 2.2 million acres (0.9 million hectares). Myanmar was losing 1.7 million acres (0.7 million hectares). Even tiny Costa Rica was losing 300,000 acres (120,000 hectares) a year. Other countries, including Haiti, Nepal, Sri Lanka and Ghana, continued to experience rapid deforestation, even though they had almost no forests left.

Opposite page: Forest fires—many human-made— have taken an enormous toll on the environment. Here, smoke clouds the sky as a forest burns in New Brunswick, Canada.

Natural Causes of Deforestation

On May 18, 1990, a monstrous explosion occurred on Mount St. Helens, a volcano in southern Washington. As pressure from the gas and molten rock inside the volcano was suddenly relieved, a blastwave of hot gas formed. Temperatures in the wave were estimated to be more than 900°F (482°C). Trees up to 16 miles (26 kilometers) away were toppled by the wave. Further on, pines and firs remained standing. But the blastwave's heat scorched these trees, turning their needles orange and weakening the trees so that many of them died. Still further afield, ash emitted during the eruption coated tree leaves, interfering with photosynthesis until rain washed the leaves clean and new growth burst from buds.

More than 100 square miles (260 square kilometers) of pines, firs, hemlocks and other trees were buried or blown down by the eruption. Animal populations were also devastated. The Washington Department of Game estimated that the casualties included 5,200 elk, 6,000 black-tailed deer, 300 bobcats, 200 black bears, 1,400 coyotes, 11,000 hares and 27,000 grouse. Some 11 million fish, including trout and young salmon, died as ash and other sediment damaged lakes and rivers. Untold millions of insects perished. Animals that survived had to cope with changed habitats and reduced food supplies.

Volcanic eruptions are one of several natural forces capable of causing extensive damage to forests. Another is violent storms, such as hurricanes or typhoons. In 1979, when Hurricane David hit the Caribbean island of Dominica, the storm's fierce winds destroyed much of the island's rain forests. Ten years later, in 1989, Hurricane Hugo struck the nearby island of Montserrat. Nicknamed the Emerald Isle because of its lush forests, Montserrat became a sea of brown after Hugo snapped off the tops of trees as if they were puny matchsticks. Several days later, Hugo hit South Carolina, causing more than $1 billion in damage to the state's timber.

Hardest hit was Francis Marion National Forest north of Charleston. Hurricane Hugo damaged or destroyed 70% of the trees in this 250,000-acre (100,000 hectare) forest. One

LIFE CYCLE OF A FOREST

Lightning strikes a dead tree, igniting an old forest.

5 weeks

Fire kills most of the trees, but some roots survive. Shrubs and grasses start to grow.

Next spring

Lodgepole pine and western larch appear first, their seeds released by the intense heat of the fire.

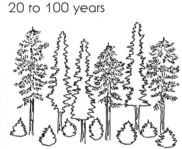

20 to 100 years

Subalpine firs grow slowly in the shade of the lodgepole and larch.

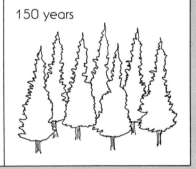

150 years

Fir trees mature and replace larch and lodgepole as dominant trees until the cycle begins again.

forester calculated that the downed timber was the equivalent of a board 1-inch thick by 12-inches wide (2.5 centimeters by 30 centimeters) long enough to circle the Earth seven times!

Also affected was the red-cockaded woodpecker, an endangered species dangerously close to extinction. The Francis Marion Forest was home to about 475 colonies of the woodpeckers, which live in cavities of mature pine trees. Only 5% of the trees in which the birds lived were undamaged. In an attempt to help the homeless birds, people carved out cavities in some of the pines that remained standing. The attempt was at least partially successful: birds settled into about half of the cavities. "It will take a very long time for the forest to recover, and at least several decades before the red-cockaded population can return to pre-hurricane levels," said Robert G. Hooper, a research biologist with the U.S. Forest Service. "But the woodpecker will be a driving factor in whatever decisions are made affecting this forest in the future."

Forest Fires

In 1990, Yosemite National Park celebrated its 100th anniversary. And for the first time in its history, part of the park was closed to visitors. The closing came during the height of the tourist season, as fire burned more than 20,000 acres (8,000 hectares) of forest. Among the casualties were centuries-old trees that had been home to rare southern spotted owls.

The Yosemite fires were started by lightning. High winds helped to spread the flames. And a lengthy drought had increased the amount of flammable brush and debris on the forest floor.

Many forest fires are caused by people's carelessness. Discarded cigarettes, untended campfires and other thoughtless acts can result in vast destruction. Such was the case in Yellowstone National Park in 1988. A fire believed to have been started by a dropped cigarette grew into the largest fire in Yellowstone's history, covering almost 500,000 acres (200,000 hectares). Meanwhile, lightning-sparked fires were also raging in Yellowstone and nearby areas; altogether, nearly 1 million acres (400,000 hectares) were damaged. Thousands of additional wildfires—some large, some small— also raged out of control in the United States during 1988, particularly in Alaska and the western states. By the time that November rain and snow finally doused most of the fires, an estimated 6 million acres (2.4 million hectares) had burned.

Forest fires destroy immeasurable amounts of valuable timber. They kill not only trees but also other organisms. They destroy needed habitats. But they may also provide

FOREST REGIONS

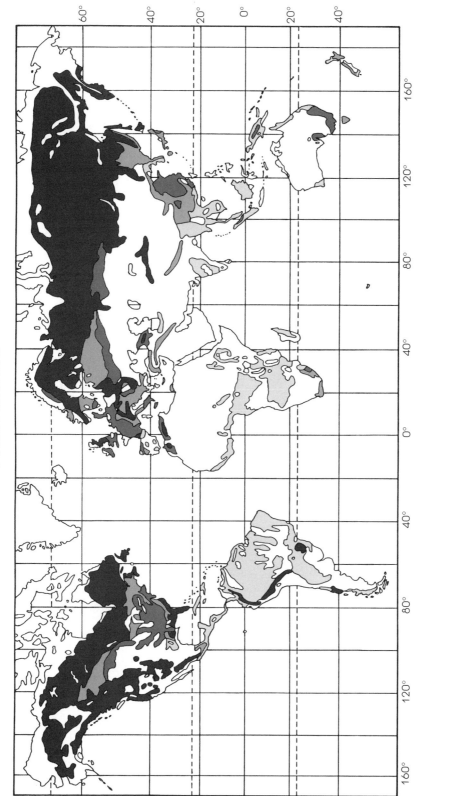

Softwoods

Hardwoods

Mixed hardwoods and softwoods

Tropical hardwoods

benefits. They destroy diseased timber and insect pests, preventing the pests from spreading to healthy trees. They open the area to sunlight needed by young plants. The ashes provide nitrogen and other nutrients needed by both surviving trees and new growth.

Many healthy trees survive fires, often because of adaptations that protect them against the heat and flames. Ponderosa pines, for example, have 2-inch- (5-centimeter-) thick bark that insulates the living cells. Sequoias have a fire-resistant bark. They also store huge amounts of water in their trunks, which helps them withstand fire. In years when rainfall is plentiful, a large sequoia may store up to 1,000 gallons (3,785 liters) of water.

Some trees that are weakened by fire respond by producing exceptionally large numbers of cones and seeds, thereby increasing the chances of creating a new generation. Aspens grow long horizontal roots that give rise to many sprouts after a fire. These sprouts grow to form extensive stands of new trees. Lodgepole pines and western larch produce cones that open and release their seeds only in the intense heat of a fire. Once released, the seeds quickly sprout, forming the first new trees in the burned area. A year after the 1988 fires in Yellowstone, young lodgepole pines were already 2 inches (5 centimeters) tall.

Young lodgepole pines and larch cannot grow well in shade, but they thrive in sunlight. As they grow and begin to create shade, they provide a habitat for the next generation of firs, which cannot grow well in sunlight. As the decades pass, a mature forest forms. Debris collects on the forest floor, and slowly the stage is set for another fire. Most of the forests that burned in Yellowstone in 1988 were 200 to 300 years old. They began to grow after fires swept through the area in the 1700s. Now, new forests are forming; the cycle is being repeated.

Pests and Diseases

Trees, like all organisms, are attacked by a wide range of pests and diseases. These include bacteria, fungi, viruses, insects, mites and other organisms. In general, trees in cooler climates are more vulnerable to pests and diseases than trees in forests near the equator. Forests in cooler climates lack the great diversity of species found in tropical forests. With little diversity, it is easier for a disease to spread from one tree to another tree of the same species than it is in a forest with many different kinds of trees.

Often, tree diseases are spread by people, perhaps as diseased lumber is shipped from one place to another or as pests hitch rides on cars and trucks. Among the most destructive tree diseases of the 20th century has been Dutch elm disease. The disease was first identified in the Netherlands around 1920. By 1926 it was recorded in England. Four years later, having been accidentally introduced into North America, cases were seen near Cleveland, Ohio. Dutch elm disease has killed millions of elms in Europe and North America. The disease is caused by a fungus that plugs up the xylem and phloem, preventing the movement of food and water within the tree. The tree wilts and gradually dies. The fungus is generally spread by bark beetles. These beetles carve tunnels under the bark of trees. If they burrow in diseased elms, they become contaminated with the fungus. Then, when they crawl onto healthy elms and begin to feed, they transmit the fungus.

Another destructive fungus causes a disease called chestnut blight. Accidentally introduced into North America from Asia, it has almost completely wiped out the American chestnut tree. This species once accounted for 25% of the trees in the northeastern United States. About 40% of the tallest trees in deciduous forests south of the Ohio River were American chestnuts. The trees were a major source of timber; the dense wood was used for everything from furniture to railroad ties. In the autumn, people would collect and eat the tasty nuts. Chestnut blight was first identified in New York City in 1904. Each year, its range expanded, killing almost every tree in its path. Today, the American chestnut is seldom seen in forests. People are unfamiliar with the taste of its nuts and its wood is too rare to be of commercial value.

ATTACK OF THE GYPSY MOTHS

It was a clear, starry night. Nonetheless, there was a steady drizzle. It sounded like rain, but it was the fall of caterpillar droppings. Thousands upon thousands of dark, hairy caterpillars were chewing, chewing, chewing. They had eaten all the leaves on the oak trees. Now they were gobbling up maple leaves, pine needles and every other kind of leaf.

Gypsy moths have been among the worst pests in the northeastern United States and neighboring parts of Canada. In 1981, at the peak of their activity, they defoliated millions of acres of trees. Some of the trees survived. But many died, particularly evergreens and trees weakened by disease and old age.

The life cycle of the gypsy moth has four stages: egg, caterpillar, pupa and adult. The eggs are laid in summer. The female moth lays a pale, fuzzy mass that contains between 100 and 1,000 eggs. The eggs hatch into tiny caterpillars the following spring.

As the days got sunnier and warmer, the caterpillars begin to climb up the trees or other objects on which they were born. As they climb, they secrete a trail of thin silk threads. They climb as high as possible. Then the caterpillars drop off, continuing to secrete silken threads and dangling in midair until they are carried by the wind to a new location. This method of traveling from place to place is be-

lieved to be the reason why the insects are called "gypsy" moths.

After the caterpillars have dispersed, they begin to eat. They grow bigger and bigger—and eat more and more. A single gypsy caterpillar devours up to 40 square inches (260 square centimeters) of leaves.

In early July, the caterpillars stop eating. They crawl under flaps of bark and into other protected places, where they change into pupae. In the pupal stage, the caterpillars turn into adult moths. This process takes about two weeks. The adult moths have only one purpose: to reproduce. They do not eat. They mate and the females lay eggs; then they die. The eggs ensure that the cycle will begin again.

Gypsy moths have enemies. Birds and mammals are important predators. Frogs eat larvae and adults. Ground beetles, which are good climbers, feed on larvae and pupae. Several kinds of wasps and flies are parasites on larvae or pupae. At

times when the gypsy moth population explodes, however, these enemies are unable to prevent widespread damage.

In 1989, another enemy of the gypsy moth was discovered: a fungus. Scientists realized that this wasn't a new enemy but one that had been around for many years. They identified it as *Entomophaga maimaiga*. This fungus had been brought to the United States from Japan, where it effectively controls gypsy moth populations. The Japanese strain was released in Massachusetts in 1910. Apparently, it took almost 80 years for the fungus to adapt to its new habitat and become an effective pest of gypsy moths in the United States.

Scientists hope to develop the fungus as a biological weapon to control gypsy moths. It could be sprayed on trees when gypsy moth populations explode. This would not eradicate all gypsy moths. But it would keep the gypsy moth population at low levels, so they would cause only minimal damage to trees.

Fuel Wood

More than 2 billion people in developing countries depend on wood for cooking and heating. But the amount of wood collected is greater than the annual growth. Thus fuel wood has become harder and harder to find, and collecting enough wood takes more and more time. According to a study, commissioned by the U.S. Office of Technology Assessment (OTA), in some countries it takes up to 300 person-days of work to meet one household's annual fuel wood needs. (A person-day of work is the work done by one person in one day).

The difficulties in collecting wood has caused dramatic changes in the lives of many poor people. For example, according to the OTA study, many families in Upper Volta now eat only one cooked meal a day. In Senegal, families have replaced slow-cooking grains such as millet with quicker-cooking but less nutritious grains such as rice.

In parts of Africa and Asia, fuel wood shortages have forced people to burn animal dung and agricultural wastes—materials that otherwise would be used to fertilize farmland. As a result, the land produces fewer crops. It has been estimated that if the cow dung burned for fuel in developing countries was used for fertilizer, grain production could increase by 20 million tons a year.

Clearing the Land

Each year, people cut millions of acres of forests for lumber, paper and other wood products. In some places, particularly Europe, virgin forests have long been replaced by carefully managed forests. Cutting is balanced by reforestation. In other places, including most tropical areas and western North America, overcutting occurs. Forests are being cut down faster than they can be replaced by new forests.

In the tropics, at least 12.3 million acres (5 million hectares) of forests are cut annually for hardwood—an area the size of Vermont and New Hampshire. About half the wood is used within the country of origin. The remainder is exported. Many tropical countries owe huge amounts of

20 TONS AN ACRE

During the Vietnam War, the United States sprayed more than 100 million tons of herbicides and defoliants over 5 million acres (2 million hectares) of croplands and forests in Vietnam. The purpose of this rain of poison was to deny opposition forces food and jungle cover under which to hide. Herbicides kill plants directly. Defoliants cause plants to drop their leaves.

If plants are repeatedly sprayed with defoliants, as were the plants in many Vietnamese forests, the plants will eventually die.

In addition, during the Vietnam War the United States destroyed large areas of forests by dense bombing and by bulldozing and plowing. Most of Vietnam's forests have not recovered from the war. Wildlife has not returned and crop productivity remains low.

Warfare has also destroyed forests elsewhere in the world. Other military activities also threaten forests. A number of Latin American countries, for example, have constructed highways, airstrips and other development projects in border areas for "national security."

money to foreign banks and governments. By exporting timber, they obtain money to pay these debts. In the 1980s, for example, Indonesia was cutting up to 2.5 million acres (1 million hectares) of forest a year. Exports of much of this timber earned the country well over $1 billion a year.

The largest importer of tropical hardwood is Japan, which has few forests. The second largest importer is the United States. In both the tropics and the importing nations, the wood is used mostly to build houses. The paper industry—the other major wood user—uses primarily softwood. The United States and Canada are the main producers of softwood. Many tropical nations import paper, or import softwood pulp from which to make paper. According to the U.S. Office of Technology Assessment: "This is likely to change in the next few decades. New technologies . . . make it possible to produce high-quality paper pulp from 100% hardwoods and from a mixture of many hardwood species."

In the tropics, removal of lumber is often followed by the creation of farms and ranches. In most cases, however, farmers and ranchers don't bother to harvest the timber as they clear land. Instead, they simply burn the wood. In 1988, photographs taken by satellites orbiting the Earth recorded 170,000 fires in the western Amazon—fires started by peasants and ranchers. At times the smoke over the capital of the state of Rondonia, Porto Velho, grew so dense that the airport had to be shut down. By the end of the year, an estimated 12,350 square miles (32,000 square kilometers) of Brazilian rain forest were reduced to ashes.

The peasants were practicing a form of farming called slash-and-burn agriculture. They cleared the land, then planted their crops. Tropical soils contain few nutrients, however. They quickly lose their fertility. In several years, the soil is exhausted and harvests are poor. The peasants abandon the farm, move deeper into the forest and slash and burn another parcel of land.

Forest lands cleared for cattle ranches also are productive for only a few years. Erosion and other problems soon make the land useless. Like the peasants, the ranchers abandon the land and clear another section of forest.

Large development projects sponsored by national governments and often supported by financial aid from other countries have frequently been undertaken with little or no consideration of their effects on the environment. Roads have been built through forests to enable settlers and loggers to reach previously inaccessible lands. Hydroelectric dams and mines are other projects that frequently result in the destruction of large areas of forest.

Many of these projects were designed to provide employment and improved living conditions for growing numbers of poor people. But all too often the end results have been devastated forests, ruined soils—and continued poverty.

Air Pollution

Air pollution has become a major cause of forest loss. Instead of the quick death by a logger's saw, the death caused by air pollution is slow. Over a period of years, pollutants accumulate in the tree's cells. The cells become weakened. This makes the tree more susceptible to insect attacks, disease and drought—much like a person whose lungs have been weakened from breathing in smoke and other pollutants becomes more susceptible to lung cancer and other respiratory diseases.

As a tree becomes stressed, growth slows. Leaves and needles turn yellow and drop prematurely from branches. Roots cease to absorb water and nutrients.

Some tree species—and even some varieties within a species—are more sensitive than others to pollution. The overall health of trees is another factor: Trees already under stress from drought or pest damage are more susceptible to pollution than are healthy trees. Age may be a factor, too. Young seedlings are especially susceptible to injury from smog.

Forest damage from air pollution is visible in most parts of the world. The damage is particularly severe in Europe. More than half the trees in the British Isles, the Swiss Alps and western Germany are dead or seriously damaged. Czechoslovakia has lost more than 80,000 acres (32,000 hectares) of forests. Large patches of Poland's forests have been destroyed; researchers estimate that by the end of the 1990s more than half of Poland's 32,000 square miles (83,000 square kilometers) of forests will be damaged.

In North America, forests are also suffering severe damage, particularly in the east. Among the habitats that have been closely watched by scientists is Camels Hump, a mountain in northwestern Vermont. When Tom Siccama, a student at the University of Vermont, studied the mountain's vegetation in the mid-1960s, the upper slopes were covered with dense forests of red spruce and balsam firs. Some of the spruce were more than 300 years old. Today, many of those trees are gone. Between 1965 and 1985, 50% of the red spruce at high elevations died. More have died since then. Many of the firs are sick. Development of seedlings has declined by 50%. Instead of a lush, healthy forest, there are clusters of graying tree skeletons; the ground is littered with brown needles, broken branches and toppled trees. Scientists believe the damage has been caused by pollution that originated hundreds of miles away, at power plants and factories in the midwestern states.

It is true that some air pollution results from natural processes such as forest fires and volcanic eruptions. Almost all the pollutants that are causing today's serious problems, however, are produced by human activities. Hundreds of millions of tons of air pollutants are emitted by human activities each year. In industrialized nations, the biggest source of these pollutants is the burning of fossil fuels, especially coal and oil. Almost all cars and other vehicles use fossil fuels. Stationary sources such as power plants, factories and home-heating and cooking systems are also major consumers of fossil fuels.

Another important source of air pollution, particularly in developing countries, is the burning of living material, or biomass. This includes the deliberate burning of forests in tropical lands, the burning of agricultural wastes left over after harvests, the annual burning of grasslands to improve grazing and the burning of wood and other materials for cooking and heating.

Numerous complex interactions occur among pollutants. Many of these interactions are not yet understood by scientists. Because of the interactions, however, it is difficult to single out any one pollutant or type of pollution as the cause of a particular forest's decline. Nonetheless, two forms of air pollution appear to be the main culprits: ozone and acid rain. Individually, each does great harm. Working together they cause even more damage. For example, ozone breaks down the waxy surfaces of conifer needles. This allows acids to reach the inner cells, where they leach, or remove, nutrients.

Ozone

Ozone is a form of oxygen. Unlike ordinary oxygen, which has two atoms per molecule, ozone has three atoms per molecule. The extra atom makes a big difference. Plants and animals need ordinary oxygen to live. But were they to breathe more than a trace of ozone, they would die. Ozone is poisonous even in small concentrations. In humans, it causes breathing problems, particularly among young children, the elderly and people with asthma and other respiratory ailments. It can also cause chest pains and coughing in joggers

THE OZONE LAYER

At ground level, ozone is a killer. High in the atmosphere, it is a life-saver. The greatest concentration of ozone occurs in a layer some 10 to 30 miles (16 to 48 kilometers) above the Earth's surface. This high-altitude ozone absorbs deadly ultraviolet radiation emitted by the sun. It prevents almost all the harmful radiation from reaching the Earth's surface.

In the 1980s, scientists discovered that the ozone layer is becoming thinner. Chemicals from human activities are destroying the high-altitude ozone. As a result, increased amounts of ultraviolet radiation are reaching the Earth's surface, threatening the health of humans, animals and plants.

For example, research has shown that ultraviolet radiation can interfere with photosynthesis. In an experiment on soybeans, biologist Alan F. Teramura of the University of Maryland increased ultraviolet radiation equal to that which would result from a 25% loss of ozone. He caused a 20% to 25% drop in plant yield. If all crops were to suffer similar decreased yields, starvation in many parts of the world could result. If trees were similarly affected, wood production would dramatically fall because trees would grow much more slowly.

and other people who exercise strenuously. Research with animals indicates that long-term exposure to high ozone levels may cause permanent damage to the lungs.

Ozone forms when sunlight causes chemical reactions between nitrogen oxides and hydrocarbons. It is the major component of smog—a term derived by combining the words *smoke* and *fog*.

Some 23 million tons of ozone-producing chemicals are released each year in the United States, mostly from motor vehicles and electric power plants that burn fossil fuels. Some of the severest forest damage caused by ozone pollution has occurred in the San Bernardino Mountains. The mountains lie about 100 miles (160 kilometers) east of Los Angeles, a city infamous for its frequent, thick smog. Winds blowing off the Pacific Ocean carry the smog inland, to the slopes of the mountains. As early as the 1950s it was evident that the smog was damaging the mountains' pine tree forests. As pollution became worse and worse over the following years, more and more trees weakened and died. Thousands have been killed, mostly on the western slopes, which receive higher doses of the poisonous smog than do the eastern slopes.

Until recently, it was believed that ozone pollution was primarily a problem in countries like the United States, where the burning of fossil fuels is greatest. However, data collected in recent years indicates that ozone levels over parts of unindustrialized West Africa are as high as those over many heavily industrialized parts of the United States. High ozone levels have also been recorded over South America, particularly Brazil, and over Indonesia. The reason: biomass burning.

Acid Rain

When an acid dissolves in water, hydrogen ions are released. Hydrogen ions are single atoms of hydrogen with a positive electrical charge. The stronger the acid, the greater the number of hydrogen ions released. Acid strength, or acidity, is expressed in terms of pH. The pH scale ranges from 0 to 14. A neutral substance, such as pure water, has a pH of 7. An alkaline, or basic substance, has a pH of more than 7. An acid has a pH of less than 7. The lower the pH, the stronger the acid. Rainwater with a pH of 6 is only mildly acidic. Rainwater with a pH of 2 is as acidic as lemon juice.

The pH scale is logarithmic. This means that each increase or decrease of one pH represents a tenfold change in acidity. Lemon juice is 10 times as acidic as vinegar, which has a pH of about 3, and 100 times as acidic as tomato juice, which has a pH of about 4.

Rainfall is naturally somewhat acidic, with a pH of slightly less than 6. This acidity occurs because some carbon dioxide in the atmosphere combines with cloud droplets to form weak carbonic acid. In addition, volcanic eruptions emit acidic compounds into the air, thereby increasing the acidity of precipitation. To some degree, this natural acidity is balanced by natural sources of alkaline compounds, such as wind-blown soil, which raise the pH of precipitation.

Acid rain is usually defined as precipitation with a pH less than 5.6. Any form of precipitation may be acidic—not only rain but also snow, sleet, fog and mist. Acids can also be deposited as dry microscopic particles. Therefore, while *acid rain* is the popular term for this type of pollution, the term *acid deposition* is generally preferred by scientists.

In many parts of the world, the annual average pH of precipitation is now between 4.5 and 4.0. Much stronger acid rain has been recorded, however. Norway has recorded rainfalls with a pH of about 2. Wheeling, West Virginia, has had rain measuring 1.5—almost as acidic as battery acid!

In the industrial world, the main source of acid rain is the burning of coal and oil. These fossil fuels contain sulfur and nitrogen. During combustion, the sulfur and nitrogen combine with oxygen to form oxides, which are released into the atmosphere. Sulfur dioxide is emitted primarily from electric power plants, smelters and other stationary sources that burn coal. Nitrogen oxides are produced primarily by electric power plants and motor vehicles. In the atmosphere, the sulfur dioxide and nitrogen oxides react with water. Sulfuric acid and nitric acid are formed. Eventually, the acids fall to the ground, usually as part of precipitation.

Huge amounts of sulfur dioxide and nitrogen oxides are produced by human activities. A single power-plant smoke-stack may emit 500 tons of sulfur dioxide a day! Each year, millions of tons of sulfuric acid and nitric acid fall onto the United States. Millions of additional tons fall onto Canada, Europe and other lands. Developing countries such as the Ivory Coast in Africa and Brazil in South America are recording acidity levels equal to those in many parts of the industrial world. Much of the acid falling on these countries

WALDSTERBEN

Widespread yellowing and loss of conifer needles were first noticed in western Germany in the late 1970s. By 1982, 8% of the trees there showed signs of damage. By 1987, the figure had jumped to 52%. The phenomenon was given a name Waldsterben, or "forest death."

Germans were horrified by what was happening to their beloved forests. "When old trees die, like old people who die, well, that is sad," said forester Gerrit Mueller. "But when young people or young trees die in great numbers, that is catastrophic."

One of the most severely damaged areas in Germany has been the forest of Fichtelgebirge in northeastern Bavaria. In 1978, it was filled with tall, healthy Norway spruce. Now, almost all the trees are dead.

Ernst-Detlef Schulze and other ecologists from the nearby University of Bayreuth tried to determine the exact mechanism that caused death in Fichtelgebirge. They found that many agents were involved in the process. Nitrogen and sulfur pollutants from industry and motor vehicles began the process. These formed acid rain, which made the forest soil increasingly acidic. As the acidity rose, aluminum, which had been harmlessly present in soil minerals, became soluble—and poisonous. The aluminum prevented roots from absorbing water and nutrients needed by the trees.

Schulze also recorded unusually high concentrations of ammonium compounds and ions in the Fichtelgebirge soil. (An ion is an electrically charged atom or group of atoms.) Schulze found that, when given a choice, spruce roots will absorb ammonium rather than nitrates. Both ammonium and nitrates contain the nitrogen needed by trees for growth. Unlike nitrates, however, ammonium interferes with a tree's absorption of magnesium. Meanwhile, the unused nitrates undergo reactions that further increase soil acidity.

Gradually, the trees developed serious deficiencies of certain nutrients, including magnesium and calcium. "Had all nutrients become equally deficient, spruce trees probably could have adjusted by retarding their growth," reported Schulze. Instead, the trees were severely weakened by the chemical imbalance. Thereafter, it was a rather easy matter for fungi, insects, drought, ice storms and other secondary factors to deliver the fatal blow.

Schulze noted that efforts are being made to limit acid rain by controlling emissions from buildings and vehicles that burn fossil fuels. But he pointed out that the amount of ammonium released into the atmosphere is increasing—from sewage treatment plants, the fertilization of farmland with manure and other practices. This trend must also be reversed if healthy forests of today are to be saved from Waldsterben.

SHRINKING FORESTS
The Problems

Much of the Earth's forests are destroyed each year by fires and natural disasters.

AN ALARMING LOSS OF FORESTS IS OCCURRING all over the world. Some forests are being destroyed by natural events, such as violent storms and lightning-sparked fires. Most deforestation, however, is the result of human activities. People destroy forests to create land for farms, houses, roads and other developments. They cut down trees for firewood, lumber, paper and other forest products. They kill trees when pollutants from their factories and automobiles form smog and acid rain. The destruction of forests has numerous impacts—on wildlife, soil, water resources and even climate and weather

Left: A lumberman cuts down a giant balsam fir. *Above:* A tropical rain forest in Costa Rica lies barren after being cleared for use as pasture.

Above: The charred remains of a forest line the hills surrounding Mount St. Helens in Washington. *Right:* Production of newspapers and other printed matter uses vast amounts of paper each day.

A VOLCANIC ERUPTION such as the one that blew the top off Mount St. Helens can consume vast numbers of trees. But the number of trees destroyed by such an eruption pales when compared to the number of trees destroyed for business and industry. Building a typical American house may use wood from 25 tall Douglas fir trees. Each week, printing the Sunday edition of America's newspapers requires the equivalent of more than 500,000 trees.

Twisting crevices carved by thousands of years of erosion create an eerie landscape in New Mexico.

TREE ROOTS ATTACH TIGHTLY TO GRAINS OF SOIL, helping to anchor the tree and preventing the soil from being washed away by falling rain or melting snow. When forests are cut, the soil is exposed. It then washes or blows away. As a result precipitation runs off quickly, causing erosion and floods. In many places, particularly in poor countries, crop yields are falling dramatically because of soil erosion caused by deforestation.

DEFORESTATION THREATENS NUMEROUS SPECIES of plants and animals with extinction. In China, for example, pandas are confined to ever-shrinking forests. There is not enough bamboo to feed more than small populations of pandas. As animal populations shrink, it becomes difficult for the animals to mate and reproduce.

A giant panda chews on the branches of a bamboo plant.

forms from nitric oxide and other gases emitted during the burning of vegetation.

Winds can carry acids hundreds or even thousands of miles from the place where the pollutants were created. The acid rain that has destroyed trees atop Camels Hump in Vermont originated in the Ohio River Valley region. About half of the sulfuric acid deposited in eastern Canada has also been traced to this region. Sulfuric acid falling on northern Finland originated at large nickel and fertilizer plants in the Soviet Union. Acids that fall on Norway and Sweden originate in England, France, Germany, Austria and Italy.

The distance traveled by much acid rain has actually increased in recent decades. The cause: An anti-pollution device! In an effort to clean dirty air in industrial and urban areas, tall smokestacks were built at power plants and other facilities. The smokestacks disperse pollutants higher into the atmosphere than do shorter smokestacks. This enables prevailing winds high in the atmosphere to carry the pollutants further away from their source. But the pollutants do not disappear—they simply fall somewhere else. The International Nickel Company replaced three short stacks at its smelter near Sudbury, Ontario, with a 1,250-foot (381-meter) tall superstack in 1972. As a result, almost all the sulfur and 40% of the heavy metals emitted travel more than 37 miles (60 kilometers) from the smelter.

Some trees are more sensitive than others to acid deposition. Among the most susceptible are coniferous trees such as spruce and fir. They die if the soil is too acidic. Some soils contain alkaline substances such as calcium carbonate. These act as buffers against acid damage. The alkaline substances react with and neutralize the acids. In many mountainous areas, however, soils are thick and lack alkaline substances; elsewhere, the buffering capacity of soils has been used up. Acids that fall on these soils are not neutralized. Instead, they react with other chemicals in the soils. The acids remove compounds needed by plants for growth, and they release substances that are poisonous to the plants.

6

THE EFFECTS OF DEFORESTATION

Stand a row of dominoes on end, then push the first one. As it falls, a chain reaction occurs and all the dominoes collapse. This "domino effect" is a frequent result of deforestation. One effect creates additional effects. The people in Manaus, a city on the Amazon River in Brazil, learned this lesson as most environmental lessons are learned: the hard way. The people once depended on fish caught in the Amazon River for much of the protein in their diets. The fish, in turn, depended on the forest that surrounded Manaus. Each year, the river flooded the forest. Some of the fish would swim among the bases of trees, feeding on seeds and fruit. During the 1970s, the forests around Manaus were cut down. The fish population, deprived of one of its main food sources, declined. The people of Manaus lost a basic, inexpensive source of protein.

Some effects of deforestation are direct and swift—for example, the death of thousands of animals as their homes are burned. Other effects occur soon after the forest is cut down—for example, the loss of soil, coupled with downstream flooding. Still other effects take years or even decades to become apparent—for example, the gradual warming of the Earth's atmosphere. All of these have serious consequences. All act like falling dominoes that in turn cause other dominoes to fall.

Opposite page: Severe flooding is one terrible consequence of deforestation. Here, a boat sails on floodwater that has covered crop fields and destroyed more than 70,000 tons of rice in Bangladesh.

Declining Wildlife Populations

Loss of forests means loss of habitats for unknown millions of species. The most serious problems are occurring in tropical rain forests, which have the greatest diversity of life. The great variety of life in those forests is almost beyond the comprehension of people who live in more temperate climates. For instance, one wildlife preserve in Peru contains more bird species than are found in the entire United States. The tiny country of Panama has as many species of plants as the entire continent of Europe. Terry L. Erwin, an ecologist with the Smithsonian Institution, collected 1,200 different species of beetles from 19 specimens of one kind of tree in Panama—and 43 species of ants from a single tree in Peru.

Some scientists fear that tropical rain forests will be gone by the middle of the 21st century. If they disappear, so will at least half the species on Earth. Already, the rate of extinction is much higher than at any time since people first appeared on the Earth. The noted Harvard University biologist Edward O. Wilson calculated that the Earth may be losing as many as 17,500 species annually. According to the International Council for Bird Preservation, more than 1,000 of the 9,000 known species of birds are at risk of extinction—three times more than in the late 1970s. Other conservationists estimate that at least 25,000 of the world's estimated 250,000 species of plants are endangered. Some scientists fear that without dramatic changes in human activities, several hundred extinctions *per day* may occur by early in the 21st century.

Frequently, a combination of human activities leads to diminished plant and animal populations. For example, as the Amazon rain forest is cut down, the monkeys that live there have smaller habitats. They also become easier targets for hunters, who kill the monkeys for food or trap them for sale as pets, zoo specimens or research animals.

One reason why loss of tropical forests has such a dramatic effect on species is that many organisms that live in the forests are endemic to a single area. That is, they do not live anywhere else. Some live on only one island or one mountain range. For example, about 80% of the 3,000 flowering plant

BYE, BYE BIRDIES

For 30 years, bird watchers regularly counted breeding songbirds in Glover-Archbold Park in Washington, D.C. "The results are shocking," noted David Wilcove, senior ecologist for The Wilderness Society. "Acadian flycatchers, northern parulas, American redstarts and hooded warblers—all of which once nested there—have disappeared. Red-eyed vireos have declined more than 60%."

Dramatic declines in the populations of many species of songbirds have been recorded throughout the eastern United States and Canada. Between 1978 and 1987, northern orioles declined by 26%, wood thrushes by 31%, yellow-billed cuckoos by 37%, Tennessee warblers by 67% and bay-breasted warblers by 79%.

The greatest declines have occurred among migrating songbirds that live in forests. They spend the spring and summer months in the United States and Canada. In autumn they fly south to the Caribbean and Central and South America, where they remain until spring returns. Most ecologists believe that the loss of forests in both summer and winter homes is a major cause of the decline.

"To enter a woods on a sunny May morning and *not* hear the songs of warblers, vireos, and thrushes is a profoundly sad experience," observed Wilcove. In addition to the pleasure we derive from watching and listening to these birds, there are important ecological benefits. Songbirds eat large quantities of insects, helping to keep pest populations under control. They also pollinate flowers, shrubs and trees.

species on the Pacific island of New Caledonia are endemic. Almost half of all the bird species found on Papua New Guinea are endemic. Almost 25% of the bird species in Indonesia are endemic. This rarity makes the species particularly vulnerable to extinction.

Organisms in temperate forests are also threatened as their habitats are destroyed. At the beginning of the 1990s, the northern spotted owl became one of the most famous animals in the United States as environmentalists battled to save its habitat in the old growth forests of the Pacific Northwest. These forests once covered some 15 million acres (6 million hectares). During the past century, 80% of the forests were cut down. Today, the remaining old growth is found almost entirely on public lands. During the 1980s, the U.S. Forest Service allowed timber companies to cut record amounts of the ancient trees from national forests. As a result, the population of the northern spotted owl reached critically low levels. The National Audubon Society estimated that perhaps no more than 2,600 pairs remained in the entire Pacific Northwest. At least 17 other species may depend on the old-growth forests for breeding and foraging. Finally in 1990, pressure from environmentalists forced the U.S. Fish and Wildlife Service to list the northern spotted owl as a threatened species. This required the government to prepare a management plan to curb logging and provide protection for the bird. This may result in preventing logging in several million acres of public forests. However, the battle was far from won, for President George Bush and his staff proposed to change the U.S. Endangered Species Act and to delay restrictions on logging.

When European settlers first arrived in Australia, koalas lived throughout almost the entire continent. Gradually, they vanished from more and more places and their numbers dwindled. Today, the koala is at risk of becoming an endangered species. Between 1940 and 1990, the koala population fell from several million to less than 400,000. This furry animal lives in eucalyptus trees and feeds almost entirely on eucalyptus leaves and shoots. Nearly 80% of the koala's natural habitat has been destroyed by farms, tourist facilities and other kinds of human development along the east coast. Disease is another threat. So are automobiles: being struck by cars is a common cause of death of koalas.

Biological Diversity

Each species is biologically unique. Its genetic makeup—that is, the inherited characteristics that are passed from one generation to the next—is different from the genetic makeup of every other species.

When a species becomes extinct, its uniqueness is lost. Any benefits it might provide to people are lost. Perhaps it makes chemicals that could be used as medicines or pesticides. Perhaps it is a wild variety of a domesticated crop, with characteristics that could improve the crop. Perhaps it could be a source of fuels.

Recent history is filled with examples of valuable organisms that had been unknown to most people. Few are proving to be more important than the winged bean. The winged bean has been cultivated by forest people in Papua New Guinea for centuries. But until the 1970s, few people outside Southeast Asia had heard of the plant. Then in 1974 a research committee of the U.S. National Academy of Sciences "discovered" the plant. They reported on the highly nutritious, fast-growing plant in 1975. In less than a decade, it was being raised by people in more than 70 countries. Scientists had collected more than 500 types of winged beans in Thailand, 300 in Bangladesh and more than 100 in Indonesia. This great variety provided the possibility of creating even better crops through cross-breeding and other genetic techniques (see Chapter 8).

Changing Climate

The loss of forests, particularly tropical rain forests, can have a major impact on both local and global climate. Jagadish Shukla, a professor of meteorology at the University of Maryland, used a computer to predict the effects of deforestation in the Amazon River basin. He found that removal of the forest would cause rainfall to decline more than 26%, from the current 97 inches (2.5 meters) a year to about 72 inches (1.8 meters) a year. The average temperature of the soil would rise, and there would be a decline of 30% in the amount of moisture evaporated into the local atmosphere. As a result, it would be impossible to replace the rain forest, for the forest could not survive in the new, drier climate.

Shukla's work indicated that loss of the Amazon forest would also affect climate elsewhere. As rainfall over the Amazon decreased, there would be a decrease in the amount of water carried by the river to the Atlantic Ocean. This would change the chemistry of the oceans, which would affect the organisms living there. As the chemistry and ecology of the oceans changed, there would probably be worldwide effects on climate.

Global Warming

Many scientists predict that within the next few decades the Earth's climate will be warmer than at any time in the past 1,000 years. By the middle of the next century, it may be warmer than at any time in the past 125,000 years. The problem is that human activities are pouring huge amounts of carbon dioxide and other heat-trapping gases into the atmosphere. These gases act much like the glass in a green-house. They allow the sun's energy to reach the Earth's surface, but they prevent heat given off by the Earth from escaping into space. As more and more heat is trapped, the atmosphere becomes warmer and warmer. This process is known as the greenhouse effect.

Deforestation increases carbon dioxide levels in the at-mosphere in two ways. When trees decay or are burned, they release the carbon that has been absorbed over their entire lifetime. And without the forests, carbon dioxide that would have been absorbed by trees for photosynthesis remains in the air.

Deforestation is not the only cause of increased levels of heat-trapping gases in the atmosphere. The burning of fossil fuels by motor vehicles, power plants and factories is another major cause. Fertilizers, cattle raising and the use of various chemicals also are factors.

If the Earth's temperature rises as much and as quickly as scientists fear, the environment will be seriously affected in many ways. Changing weather patterns will result. Some places will receive more rain than they do today, while other places will become much drier. The oceans will warm and expand, causing coastal areas to be flooded, perhaps permanently. Habitats of plants and animals will disappear or change in ways that make them unsuitable for native organisms.

One anticipated effect of global warming in the United States is a loss of the nation's southern forests. Also, the range of species such as sugar maples and hemlocks is expected to shrink.

Ruined, Lost Soil

Most of the soils in rain forests are not very fertile. When organisms die and decompose, the nutrients in their cells are quickly absorbed by living plants. Thus, almost all the nutrients in rain forests are locked up in living organisms, rather than in the soil. A study in the rain forest of Venezuela found that 75% of the nutrients were in living organisms, 17% were in debris and only 8% in the soil.

Because of its low nutrient content, the soil cannot support farming for more than a few years. The soil quickly loses its fertility, crop yields fall and farmers abandon the land. The barren land hardens, severely limiting the ability of wild plants to reestablish themselves. Indeed, in some cases the soil becomes so hard that it can be crushed and used as gravel for building roads.

Adding fertilizers that contain essential nutrients to the tropical soils is not a solution. The fertilizers are ineffective in most tropical soils. Phosphorus, an essential nutrient found in fertilizers, is held so tightly by certain compounds in tropical soils that plants cannot extract enough for their own use. Another problem is that fertilizers may destroy fungi called mycorrhizae, which are essential to the growth of many tropical trees. The fungi grow in the roots of the trees and help them absorb minerals and water.

Erosion and Flooding

When precipitation falls, three things may happen to the water. Some may evaporate. Some may sink into the ground. Some may run off the surface of the land, flowing downhill toward rivers and other bodies of water.

FOR TREES ONLY

"The very signs also from which we form our judgement are often very deceptive; a soil that is adorned with tall and graceful trees is not always a favorable one, except, of course for those trees."

Pliny the Elder, Roman author of *Natural History*, A.D. 77

NATURAL PROTECTORS OF THE FORESTS

Tropical forests are home to hundreds of indigenous tribes—people who have been natives of their environment for many centuries. These people know how to live in the forests. They have valuable knowledge about the plants and animals and how to use these resources without destroying them or their environment.

Brian M. Boom, a botanist at the New York Botanical Garden, studied the forest surrounding the village of Alto Ivon in Bolivia, where Chácobo Indians live. He found 91 species of trees in one small area. The Chácobo use 75 of these species in various ways. Fibers are spun into thread and used to weave fabric. Wood is used to build homes. Trunks are hollowed out to make canoes. Fruits, leaves, bark, sap and roots are eaten and used as medicine. For example, the sap of one tree species is used to relieve muscle aches.

Shrinking forests has meant shrinking populations for many of the tribes. Some countries have begun to recognize the land rights of these people. Among the leaders has been Colombia. In 1990, the Colombian government reserved half the country's Amazon territory for the Indians. The new reserve covers 69,000 square miles (179,000 square kilometers)—an area slightly larger than the state of Washington. "Colombia believes that the Indians are the natural protectors of the Amazonian ecology," said Martin von Hildebran, head of the country's Indigenous Affairs Department.

Running water is the most important agent of erosion. Rivers and streams are forms of running water. Another form is runoff—the water that flows over the land's surface, usually after a rainfall or a spring thaw.

As forests are cut down, erosion increases. No longer is there a forest canopy to increase evaporation, to lessen the impact of falling rain and to slow the melting of snow in the spring. No longer is there a massive system of tree roots to hold soil in place and to provide air pockets through which water can soak into the ground. Water runs quickly off the cleared land, carrying away soil particles.

Soil loss is particularly severe in developing countries. A single rainstorm in the tropics can wash away 75 tons of soil from an acre (0.4 hectare) of cleared land!

Studies in the Ivory Coast found that an acre of forest on a slightly sloping hillside loses 20 pounds (9 kilograms) of soil a year. But when the forest on that hillside is cut down, the same amount of rain washes away 120,000 pounds (54,400 kilograms) of soil.

Erosion, in turn, severely affects the productivity of land. In Kenya, according to Janet Welsh Brown, senior associate at the World Resources Institute: "Thanks to soil erosion caused by deforestation and other land-use changes, crop yields in some areas are expected to fall 50% to 70% by 2000. Although only 3% of Kenya is forested, fuelwood provides 74% of the country's energy."

Without the sponge effect of the forest to moderate the flow of water, it all runs off at once. Downstream there is flooding. This can cause great destruction to farms and cities. And later in the year, during periods of drought, there are no reserves of water in the upland areas. Because of deforestation, the U.S. Virgin Islands no longer has permanent streams. Rather, streams form for only a brief time after rainstorms. Water for drinking and other uses must be shipped to the Virgin Islands from Puerto Rico or desalinized from sea water at great expense. In India, largely as a result of deforestation, the area affected by annual floods grew from 60 million acres (24 million hectares) in 1950 to 100 million acres (40 million hectares) by 1980. And by 1980, floodwaters were eroding 6 billion tons of soil from India's hills each year.

Reservoirs

The soil eroded off deforested land by running water is dropped, or deposited, as the water slows down. A river carrying soil usually deposits much of the material at its mouth, where it flows into a standing body of water, such as a lake or ocean. However, if there is an obstruction in the river, sediment will be deposited on the upstream side of the obstruction. One type of obstruction is a dam.

As a result of deforestation, the reservoirs behind many dams are filling with sediment much more rapidly than expected. This has greatly shortened the useful life of the dams. In India, the rate at which sediment is building up in most reservoirs is four to six times as high as the rate expected when the dams were designed and built. Similar problems are occurring elsewhere, particularly in the Philippines, Costa Rica and other tropical countries.

Desertification

The formation of desert is a problem of growing magnitude in dry lands that have been deforested. The problem is particularly severe in the Sahel of Africa. The Sahel is a semiarid area that lies between the Sahara desert and tropical West Africa. Here, desert is being formed faster than anywhere else in the world. The countries that are affected include Niger, Mali and Burkina Faso. Deforestation is being caused mainly by population growth, inefficient cooking practices and poor agricultural practices.

The natural ecosystem in the Sahel is called a savanna or an open forest. Acacia trees are common, but they do not form a dense canopy. They allow enough light to reach the ground so that a continuous cover of tall grasses can grow. People remove the grasses to grow crops. They cut down the acacia trees for firewood, which is burned under clay pots balanced on three stones. Young trees that aren't cut by people often are killed by browsing livestock.

No longer stopped by the acacia trees and tall grasses, winds carry in sand from the Sahara. They dry out the exposed topsoil, turning it to a fine dust that mixes with the sand. Finally, the land is unable to support any type of plant life. It is abandoned; people leave to compete for other land, or they travel to cities and towns, swelling urban-poor populations.

Areas in Mexico that were once covered with rain forests are now unable to support trees. And some scientists fear that deforestation of the Amazon could lead to desertification, particularly if deforestation's effects were combined with the effects of global warming and other environmental changes.

THE REAL ISSUE IS
SPECIES SURVIVAL
CONSUMERISM & GREE
OREGON'S ANCIE
RAINFORESTS IN 20
EARTH
FIRST!

7

PROTECTING OUR FORESTS

When the first Europeans arrived in North America, they were amazed by the huge, lush forests that seemed to stretch forever and ever. Indeed, the forests stretched across most of the continent. But as the years passed, people cut more and more of the forests, destroying huge communities of wild plants and animals. By the middle of the 20th century, almost all the virgin forests had been cut from private lands. Demand grew to cut down forests under the management of government agencies. Prime habitats in national forests in the western part of the continent swiftly fell under the buzz of chainsaws. The destruction is continuing today. According to the National Audubon Society, loggers cut enough old-growth trees in the northwestern United States each year to fill a convoy of trucks 20,000 miles (32,000 kilometers) long.

This destruction will not continue much longer, if for no other reason than the country is finally running out of virgin forests. Environmentalists warn that at the present rate of cutting few virgin forests will be left in the United States early in the 21st century. Instead of rich habitats created by trees hundreds of years old, the land will be covered with mile after mile of young trees. There will be few homes for bears, bald eagles, spotted owls and other creatures. But at least there will be trees. This is unfortunately not true in many

Opposite page: Organizations of concerned individuals play a large part in making people and governments aware of environmentally harmful practices. Here, members of Earth First! demonstrate against lumbering practices.

other places where trees are cut down. Each year, the Earth's forests are getting smaller and smaller. Reversing this trend is an important objective if future generations are going to be able to enjoy the many benefits provided by forests.

Protecting existing forests involves several basic types of actions. Some forests must be protected as complete, natural ecosystems. Pollution that weakens and kills trees must be controlled. Demand for products that require destruction of forests must be limited.

Each of these steps involves controversies. How far should foresters go to protect forests against fire? Who should pay for pollution controls? Should countries with disappearing forests follow the lead of Panama, which passed a law making it illegal to cut any tree older than five years?

Individuals have important contributions to make if forests are to be saved. They can conserve energy, thus limiting pollution. They can recycle paper. They can plant and care for trees around their homes, along roadways and in parks. They can pressure governments to establish parks and other forest preserves and to enact and enforce laws that protect ecosystems and endangered species. They can ask agencies in charge of forests to explain how they are managing forests and how they plan to meet future needs. "You need citizens asking embarrassing questions," said David A. Bella, professor of engineering at Oregon State University. "They need to do their homework, but they don't have to be experts."

How Much Is Enough?

Protected habitats must be of sufficient size. They must be large enough for species to have plenty of room to live and reproduce. Some species need big areas of suitable habitat. Mountain gorillas, which once inhabited large equatorial forests of central Africa, are in great danger of extinction because their habitat has been almost completely destroyed. Mountain gorillas live in family groups of 6 to 20 members. Wholly vegetarian, they have large appetites. A 660-pound (300-kilogram) adult eats 66 pounds (30 kilograms) of leaves, shoots, bark, fruit and other plant matter a day. To find sufficient food without destroying the forest, the gorillas constantly travel. During the course of a year, the family covers an area of 30 square miles (77 square kilometers)—a large area for a relatively small number of animals.

In many places, large expanses of forest have been fragmented by human development. In the northeastern United States, for example, forests have been carved up and separated by housing developments, highways and shopping malls. Similarly, in the ancient forests of Oregon and Washington, clear-cutting large stands of ancient trees has left what the National Audubon Society called "a crazy quilt of fragmented habitat." This creates plentiful edges to the remaining forests, but diminished amounts of forest interiors. Edges and interiors form different habitats. Organisms that live in one may avoid or be unable to survive in the other. Openings between habitats may act like barricades, preventing organisms from moving from one suitable habitat to another. Research in the Amazon rain forest found that as many as 95% of the birds accustomed to the darkness of forest interiors will not cross a clearing—even to find food or to breed.

How large must a rain forest be if it is to remain a rain forest? Thomas Lovejoy, an ecologist now at the Smithsonian Institution, is trying to answer this question. In 1979, Lovejoy set up a 20-year experiment in the Amazon rain forest. Reserves of various sizes, from 2.5 to 2,500 acres (1-1,000 hectares), were established. Lovejoy quickly learned that the smallest reserves are worthless. Within months, their vegetation began to change and populations of insects, birds and mammals declined. A growing number of tropical ecologists believe that all of Lovejoy's reserves are too small. They suggest that in order to survive, a rain forest ecosystem must be at least 125,000 acres (50,000 hectares) in size. Some believe the minimum size needs to be 500,000 acres (200,000 hectares).

Providing Financial Help

Sometimes, habitats are protected by law, but the laws are not enforced. This is a particular problem in developing countries with large populations of poor people and limited financial resources. Economic pressures to cut down forests, even forests in parks, becomes intense. The U.S. Office of Technology Assessment reported in 1984: "The rapid loss of forests in most tropical countries forces people to try to establish protected areas whenever and wherever the opportunity arises regardless of whether adequate, continuing protection will be available to care for the land and its resources. Many protected areas exist only on paper and in fact continue to undergo destruction."

Part of the problem is the fact that many developing countries owe huge amounts of money to foreign governments and banks. To pay these debts, the countries often depend on their natural resources. Forests are cut down not to provide wood for local needs but to pay debts. This is a short-sighted approach, pointed out The World Commission on Envi-

EARTH FIRST!

How far should people go to protect the environment? Some people are very angry because old-growth forests continue to be destroyed at a rapid rate. They are frustrated by compromises that seem to protect big corporations rather than the environment. They are impatient with politicians and traditional environmental groups. They believe that more radical measures than letter-writing, lobbying, lawsuits and planting seedlings are needed.

One such group of people is Earth First! Founded in 1980 and active primarily in the western United States, its slogan is "No compromise in defense of Mother Earth.

Earth First! was among the first environmental groups that tried to save the nation's remaining old-growth forests. Members have appeared at rallies and demonstrations dressed as trees and spotted owls. They have held sit-ins at logging sites and sat for days on platforms suspended from threatened trees. Linking arms, they have formed circles around giant redwoods, at least momentarily preventing loggers from cutting down the 500-year-old trees. They have blocked docks, in efforts to stop shipments of timber to foreign countries.

Other tactics advocated by some Earth Firsters include dangerous acts of sabotage.

People have poured sand in the fuel tanks of logging equipment. They have driven metal spikes into trees, which can ruin loggers' saws. Such acts have been condemned by other environmental groups, who believe that sabotage hurts rather than helps the environmental cause. They worry that extreme acts will scare off potential supporters of efforts to protect the environment. But, say Earth First! supporters, if they hadn't been willing to go to extremes, saving the old-growth forests of the Pacific Northwest would not have become one of the nation's leading conservation issues.

ronment and Development: "It requires relatively poor countries simultaneously to accept growing poverty while exporting growing amounts of scarce resources."

Foreign banks and governments have often provided billions of dollars of aid to developing countries to spend on dams, roads and other large-scale projects that are very harmful to the environment. Much of the clearing of rain forests in Brazil and Indonesia was supported by money from international banks. So, too, were cattle ranches in Africa, to raise beef for export—in places where local people cannot afford to buy meat.

This is beginning to change, thanks largely to pressure from environmentalists. A small but growing portion of financial assistance provided by the United States and other industrialized countries goes directly toward projects that protect the environment. International banks have hired ecologists and begun to consider the environmental effects of projects they may finance.

Debt-for-Nature

Imagine that you are a giant bank. Ten years ago, you lent $10 million to a poor country. It is now obvious that your chances of getting the money back are very, very slim. Along comes a conservation group. It offers to buy the debt from you for $2 million. Deciding that $2 million is better than nothing, you agree to sell the IOUs. Now the poor country owes $10 million to the conservation group. But the group says it will cancel the debt if the country agrees to protect certain forests. The country sets aside the land as a giant park. It no longer has the $10 million debt—and it has preserved a precious habitat.

This, basically, is how debt-for-nature swap works. The idea was first proposed in 1984. Since then, swaps have occurred in Bolivia, Ecuador, Costa Rica, the Philippines, Zambia and Madagascar. In Bolivia, a 3.7-million acre (1.5 million hectare) rain forest preserve was created in exchange for forgiveness of a $650,000 debt. That debt had been purchased from banks by Conservation International for $100,000.

In addition to helping to establish nature preserves, the environmental organizations also provide technical assistance, training of local conservation professionals and money for managing preserves.

To Burn or Not to Burn

Fire has been called nature's cleansing act. It consumes the litter that collects on a forest floor. It kills diseased trees and insect pests, preventing their spread. It provides suitable environments for the growth of plants that need sunlight in order to sprout and develop. But forest fires are also destructive, killing valued organisms and causing billions of dollars of damage to timber and buildings. Thus, foresters face a dilemma. Should they allow natural fires to burn? Or should they fight every fire.

In Europe, many forests are carefully managed plantations. Every forest fire is fought; foresters try to put out the fire as quickly as possible. This practice was followed in the United States for almost a century, even though many U.S. forests, particularly in the western states, are large, biologically diverse wildernesses. In the 1960s, U.S. policy changed in national parks, in recognition of the important role that fire plays in forest ecosystems. Natural fires were allowed to burn unless they threatened people, property or endangered species. Generally, however, such problems did not arise. Most fires died out when they reached areas with little undergrowth and deadwood. Then came the 1988 fires in Yellowstone National Park. When the fires began, park officials let them burn. But within a few weeks, it became apparent that the fires were growing out of control. Efforts were made to suppress the fires, but it was too late. By the time the fires were finally out, nearly 1 million acres (400,000 hectares) in Yellowstone and nearby areas had been burned.

The let-it-burn policy was loudly criticized, particularly by political leaders. Many environmentalists, however, continued to feel the policy was appropriate. They pointed out that massive amounts of deadwood and debris littered the Yellowstone forests, largely because people had suppressed fires for so long. Had natural fires been allowed to burn in earlier years, so much fuel would not have collected, and the 1988 fires would not have had such a severe impact.

The environmentalists' belief that nature should be allowed to follow its course received added support the following year. "It was the most beautiful spring and summer around here in years," said Yellowstone naturalist Greg Kroll. Blackened tree trunks were surrounded by lush carpets of grass and wildflowers. Scattered among these small plants were young lodgepole pines—the first trees of what will eventually become a new forest.

Limiting Pollution and Waste

Less polluted air would clearly benefit us in many ways. In addition to protecting forests, it would improve people's health. It would save money now spent to repair bridges, buildings and car paint damaged by airborne acids. It would increase crop productivity. A recent study by the U.S. Environmental Protection Agency concluded that ozone pollution alone reduced crop yield by $2.5 billion to $3 billion a year—just in the United States!

As discussed in Chapter 5, the major air pollutants that damage trees result from the burning of fossil fuels by motor vehicles, power plants and factories. In developing countries, burning of trees, agricultural wastes and other living matter is a major cause of air pollution.

Modifying engines and installing catalytic converters reduce automobile emissions. Improved fuel economy is also valuable, not only to limit pollutants that damage trees, but to limit carbon dioxide emissions that speed global warming. Data from the Environmental Action Foundation indicate that a car averaging 18 miles per gallon (mpg) emits 58 tons of carbon dioxide over its lifetime. A car averaging 27.5 mpg emits 38 tons. A car averaging 60 mpg emits only 17 tons.

Burning "cleaner" fuels is one way to reduce pollution. Some coals contain as much as 6% sulfer, while others have only 1% sulfer—and therefore produce much less of the pollutant sulfur dioxide. Also, sulfur can be removed, or "washed," from coal before the coal is burned. Tests suggest that 90% or more of the sulfur can be removed by this process.

IMPROVEMENTS

The more efficiently a log is used, the fewer the number of trees that have to be cut to meet demand. In the United States at the beginning of the 20th century, as little as one third of a log might be converted into lumber or other useful products. The remaining two thirds were discarded. Today, American mills make much more efficient use of logs. There is almost no waste. Even the bark is used, either to make soil mulch for gardens or as a fuel, to provide energy needed to operate the pulp and paper mills.

Another method is to remove pollutants after the burning process but before they can enter the atmosphere. Devices called scrubbers are placed in smokestacks of factories and power plants that burn coal. They use a spray of water and chemicals to remove, or scrub out, pollutants. There is a negative side effect, however: scrubbers use about 5% of the energy produced by burning the coal, thus increasing coal consumption.

Developing nonpolluting energy sources is another solution. Solar energy and wind power are two alternative energy sources that are particularly attractive from an environmental standpoint.

Individuals have important roles in limiting air pollution, largely by conserving energy. By buying fuel-efficient cars and by driving less, people decrease the amount of pollution they produce. By using energy-efficient appliances and avoiding wasteful uses of electricity, they reduce the demand for the production of electricity at power plants. By recycling metal cans and other materials, they reduce the amount of energy needed to make new products. For example, making cans from recycled aluminum uses only 5% of the energy needed to make cans from virgin materials.

Solar Cookers

More efficient cooking stoves can help slow deforestation in many developing areas. One stove that requires no firewood at all is the solar oven. It depends entirely on energy from the sun to cook food. In addition to saving trees, the solar oven eliminates the dense wood smoke that is a major source of pollution in many poor communities.

William F. Lankford, a professor of physics at George Mason University, is among the people who are helping to introduce solar cooking to people in developing countries. "The oven I am working with is basically a wooden box," he explained. "There are no electrical connections, no chemicals, no fire. With the right materials and a little instruction, anyone can build a solar oven. The main components consist of a box with glass at the top to let in the sunshine and a black metal plate at the bottom to absorb the sunlight and turn it into heat. If the sides and bottom are well-insulated, the oven will easily reach temperatures above 300° F (150° C)."

The real challenge, said Lankford, was to change people's habits—to get them to switch from cooking with firewood. People also have to change recipes. "As with anything new, experience is needed to get the cooking details right," he explained. "How much water should be added to new rice? To old rice? How much more cooking time is needed for last year's beans as compared to the current harvest?

Recycling Paper

The United States is the world's largest consumer of paper and paper products. According to the American Paper Institute, Americans consumed 86 million tons of paper in 1989. About 27.6 million tons of this total were recycled. The largest portion of this consisted of used corrugated boxes; they compose about 40% of all waste paper recycled in the United States. Newspapers and office papers make up most of the remainder.

Using newspapers and other waste paper as opposed to virgin pulpwood to make paper and paperboard results in energy savings ranging from 60% to 70%. In addition, recycling paper saves trees—lots and lots of trees. If Americans recycled all their Sunday newspapers, they would save more than 500,000 trees a week!

For recycling to work, people need to also buy and use products made from recycled materials, rather than products made from virgin materials. Unless there is a market for the recycled products, manufacturers will not make those products. Greeting cards, writing paper, envelopes, books and toilet paper are among the many consumer products that can be made with recycled paper.

Even better than recycling waste paper is avoiding the creation of waste paper. This is called source reduction. A paper shopping bag can—and should—be recycled. But carrying purchases home in a reusable cloth bag is a wiser decision. A paper towel may be handy, but using a cloth towel or a sponge can easily save several rolls of paper towels a year.

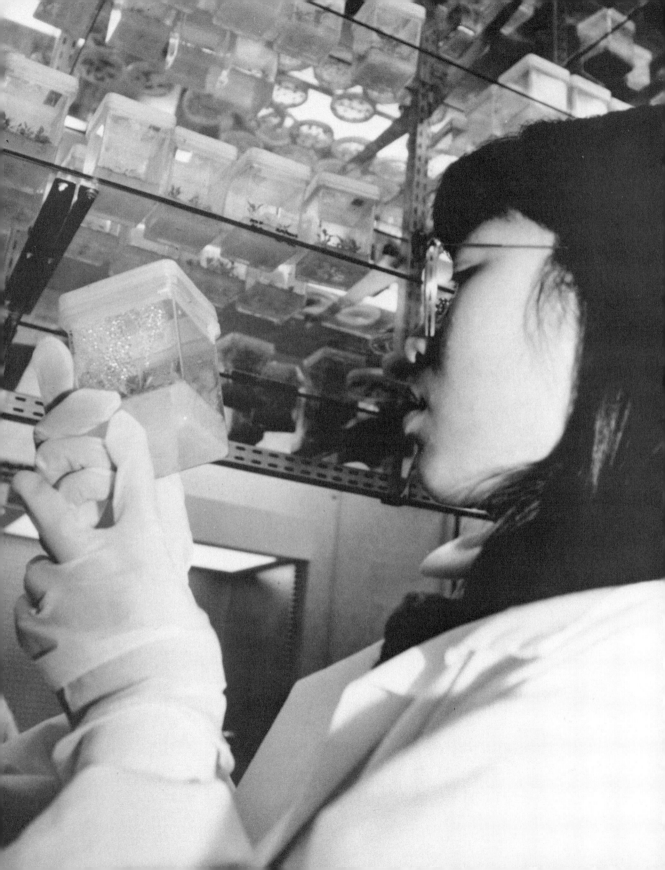

8

NEW STRATEGIES, NEW APPROACHES

The needs of forest ecosystems often seem to conflict with the needs of people. Yet a balance must be found that allows both the ecosystems and people to survive and prosper. Ways are needed to protect natural ecosystems, yet enable people to raise food and earn money for basic needs. Ways are needed to provide sufficient wood products today while ensuring that future generations will also have access to the benefits of forests.

There is much to do, and not much time left if we are to slow and reverse deforestation. Fortunately, people are testing a variety of promising new strategies and approaches. Among these are new forestry techniques and advances in genetics.

Sustainable Forestry

Many useful and valuable forest products are produced with little or no harvesting of trees. These include nonwood products obtained from trees and other vegetation: oils, drugs, chicle and other gums, turpentine, rosin, fibers and spices. Also included are important food sources: wild animals, fish, fruits, nuts, honey, fungi and vegetables. Other forest products have potential commercial value. But they are not currently being harvested, or they are only gathered on a small scale. Developing markets for these products would

Opposite page: Advances in biotechnology have enabled scientists to pursue many programs that can help to better preserve our forests. Genetic engineering, selective breeding and cloning are just a few techniques now being used to improve the survival rates of threatened trees.

provide income for people and would provide incentives to protect the forest ecosystem.

Scientists and economists are beginning to convince governments that forests can be worth much more standing than cut down. The governments are learning that a cattle ranch or farm that must be abandoned in a few years is not equal to a forest that provides marketable products for years on end. As a result, governments in Brazil and other developing countries are ending tax breaks and other subsidies to ranchers and farmers. They are setting aside large forest areas as extractive reserves. People such as rubber tappers and Brazil nut gatherers are allowed to harvest, or extract, renewable products from these reserves.

Some forest organisms might be raised by people on farms and in gardens. One example is the capybara. Capybaras are the world's largest rodents. They weigh up to 100 pounds (45 kilograms). Capybaras live on the edges of lakes, rivers and swamps in Central and South America. They eat only plants, mainly swamp grasses and aquatic plants. According to the U.S. Office of Technology Assessment, wild and semidomesticated capybaras have been eaten by people in Latin America for centuries. Only recently, however, have Venezuelans begun raising capybaras on farms. In addition to being a source of meat, capybaras are valuable for their skins. The skin can be made into leather that is valued by glovemakers because it stretches in one direction only.

Papua New Guinea

In Papua New Guinea, several economically valuable markets that depend on protecting forest habitats have been developed. The country has developed management systems to domesticate, breed and harvest a number of animal species. Large, flightless birds called cassowaries are raised for their feathers. Birds called megapodes are raised for eggs. Wallabies and deer are raised for meat and hides.

The government of Papua New Guinea has also supported the farming of crocodiles, which are a valuable source of leather. To discourage the hunting of large, wild crocodiles, the government banned the sale of large skins. Instead, it encouraged villagers to collect tiny hatchlings. Crocodiles in the wild lay from 30 to 70 eggs a year. Because of natural enemies and other perils, very few of the young crocodiles that hatch from eggs survive to adulthood in the wild. Villagers collect some of the hatchlings and raise them in captivity until they are one or two years old. The villagers receive a good income for this work. They know that they will continue to receive this income only if there are young hatchlings to be collected. Thus, they realize the importance of protecting the wild population of crocodiles, and the rain forests in which the crocodiles live.

Raising insects is another profitable activity in Papua New Guinea. Many of the country's insects are very beautiful and desirable to people all over the world who have insect collections. Indeed, the insects are so valuable that they have been declared a national resource. Papua New Guinea is the only country in the world whose constitution specifies insect conservation as a national objective. Villagers attract valuable butterflies by planting the butterflies' favorite shrubs around the edge of their fields. They also plant leafy plants that serve as food for butterfly caterpillars. "The combination provides a complete habitat for the butterflies' life cycle," explained Noel D. Vietmeyer of the National Academy of Sciences. "The farmer simply harvests specimens as time and demand allow. Because the butterflies are collected under relatively controlled conditions, they typically are of higher quality than wild-caught specimens. Consequently, the demand for poached [illegally gathered] specimens is reduced."

Trees as Crops

Like corn, wheat and other food crops, trees can be grown on farms. Tree farms that produce only one species of Christmas trees are an example. Growing a single kind of tree in an area is called monoculture. It has certain economic advantages. Space is not wasted on trees that have no economic value. All the trees reach maturity at the same time, making them easier to harvest.

Obviously, however, monoculture does not create an ecosystem with the rich biological diversity of a natural ecosystem. It has other drawbacks, too. The more complex and diverse the ecosystem, the better its protection against pests and disease. Usually, pests attack one specific kind of tree. In a forest composed of many different kinds of trees, it is comparatively difficult for pests to spread. Also, a biologically diverse forest is more likely to house enemies of the pests.

In a developing countries in Asia and Africa, there are large rubber plantations. These monocultures are very successful, and they supply most of the world's natural rubber. Attempts to develop rubber plantations in the Amazon have usually failed, however, because of disease. A leaf blight native to the Amazon area doesn't cause much damage in the rain forest, but it is very destructive in the monoculture environment. Similarly, another disease wiped out a banana plantation on the coast of Ecuador, on land that had been covered with rain forest.

One type of monoculture that has recently received a fair amount of attention in developing countries consists of plantations of fast-growing trees that can be cut to provide fuelwood. The wood can be burned to provide energy for heating, cooking and lighting, thereby reducing pressure to cut virgin forests. Or it can be converted into ethanol (ethyl alcohol) to power automobiles and other motor vehicles, decreasing the need for expensive imported fuels.

Monoculture is common in the United States, on both privately owned and public lands. Large areas in national forests have been clear-cut. That is, all the timber has been removed from the cutting areas at one time. The areas have then been planted with one or a few varieties of trees. The result is that much of the country's national forests has been turned into tree farms.

Using Genetics to Grow Trees

A tree—like every other organism—starts life as one cell. That cell grows and divides. The two new cells grow and divide. This process of cell growth and division happens over and over again. Eventually, the tree consists of trillions of cells. Why is it a tree instead of a monkey? Why are some parts of the tree leaves while other parts are roots? The answers to these questions are in the organism's genes.

Genes are the blueprints of life. They control the heredity, or traits, that are passed on to an individual from its parents. In the case of trees, as in the case of human beings, the genes occur in pairs. One gene of each pair came from the male parent, in a sperm cell. The second gene in the pair came from the female parent, in an egg cell. In the tree species, a single flower may produce both the sperm and egg. In other species, the sperm may be produced on one tree, the egg on another tree.

When the sperm fertilizes the egg, a single cell is formed. That cell possesses all the hereditary information needed to develop into a complex tree.

A tree has millions of genes. Each pair of genes has a specific function. One pair may control leaf shape. Another may "tell" a cell how to manufacture a certain chemical. Still another may determine flower color.

As scientists have learned how genes work, they have also learned how to put this knowledge to practical use. They have learned how to use genes to create new varieties of organisms. Some of their methods were actually in use even before genes were discovered. Others are new and controversial. The goals, however, are the same: to improve organisms. Researchers use genetic techniques to develop new tree strains that grow faster, taller and straighter, as well as strains that are more resistant to disease. Among their many achievements: new varieties of rubber trees that yield as much as six times more rubber than wild varieties.

Selective Breeding

Ever since people began domesticating wild plants and animals, they have used genetics. Even thousands of years ago, people used genetics as they deliberately tried to develop organisms with certain characteristics—a process now called

A CHEMICAL CODE

Genes are made up of an organic compound called deoxyribonucleic acid, or DNA. DNA has six parts: a sugar, the mineral phosphate and four special chemicals called bases. The bases are adenine (A), thymine (T), cytosin (C) and guanine (G). In 1953, two biologists figured out how the six parts fit together to form DNA. They said that DNA looks like a spiral staircase. Sugar and phosphate form the sides of the staircase. The four bases form the steps. Each step is made of two bases.

The sequence in which the bases occur in a gene determines the gene's hereditary message. The number of different arrangements is astronomical. This explains how there can be millions of different species of organisms and why there is such variety within each species—even though the genes of all living things are made up of DNA.

selective breeding. The people kept seeds for the following year's crops only from plants that weren't diseased or only from those that produced the most food. They learned how to breed different varieties for different purposes, such as grapes for making wine and grapes for eating. In time, people learned that if they bred a horse and a donkey, they would produce a mule.

It wasn't until the late 1800s, however, that the science of genetics got its start and people began to understand what happened, how it happened and why it happened. An Austrian monk named Gregor Mendel discovered the basic principles of heredity. Many advances in using selective breeding have occurred in this century, thanks to Mendel and later geneticists. Cross-breeding became common. In this process, one or more varieties within a species are carefully crossed, or bred together, to produce a new variety.

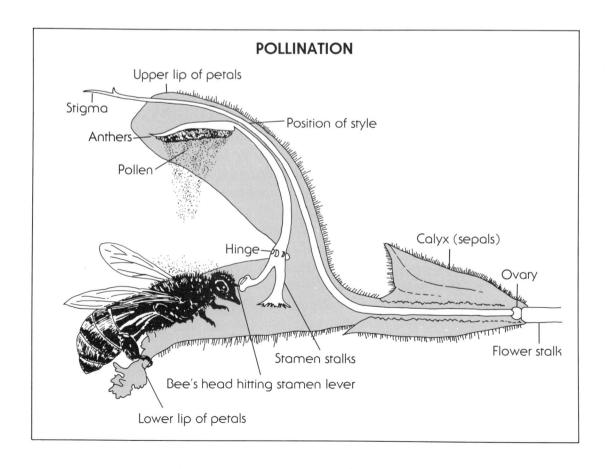

POLLINATION

Upper lip of petals

Stigma

Position of style

Anthers

Pollen

Hinge

Calyx (sepals)

Ovary

Stamen stalks

Bee's head hitting stamen lever

Flower stalk

Lower lip of petals

BAMBOO BREAKTHROUGH

Bamboos are the trees of the grass family. Among the most rapidly growing of all plants, they often reach heights of 50 feet (15 meters) or more. Some species are well over 100 feet (30 meters) tall, with stems up to 12 inches (30 centimeters) in diameter.

In Asia, bamboo forests are extremely important. The plants are put to thousands of uses. The hollow, woody stems are strong, flexible, durable and easily split lengthwise. They are used to construct houses and bridges; to make boat masts, fishing poles and furniture; as pipes and musical instruments; and to make paper, textiles and woven baskets. A secretion from the stem called tabasheer is used as a medicine to fight coughs and asthma. The grain and tender shoots, or sprouts, are eaten. The leaves are fed to livestock.

As is common with other forests, many bamboo forests are being cut faster than they can be replaced. Also, many are being destroyed and replaced with roads, houses and other types of developments.

Unfortunately, many valuable species flower and produce seeds only at intervals of 30 years or more. Some species take more than a century to reproduce. This makes it extremely difficult to replace depleted forests.

In 1990, botanists in India announced that they had developed a method to make two species of bamboo flower prematurely. In nature, the two species flower when they are 30 to 60 feet (9 to 18 meters) tall and about 30 years old. Using a "test-tube cocktail" of hormones, coconut milk and other nutrients, the botanists got plants to flower and produce seeds when they were only a few weeks old and several inches tall.

The technique is expected to allow faster replacement of depleted bamboo forests. It also opens up a range of exciting possibilities for geneticists. It speeds the ability to cross-breed species. Botanists can also insert foreign genes into reproductive cells, and more quickly learn if the insertions had the desired effects. New kinds of bamboo that grow faster and that resist disease are among the hoped-for results.

For instance, to cross-breed two varieties of apple tree, sperm nuclei produced by pollen grains from one variety (A) must fertilize egg cells from the second variety (B). So a farmer takes the pollen from a blossom on a tree of variety A and places it on the female part of a blossom on a tree of variety B. The seeds that are produced it is hoped contain the best features of both varieties. Perhaps variety A produces lots of fruit and variety B is resistant to a particular disease. By cross-breeding the varieties, the farmer hopes to create a variety that produces lots of fruit *and* is disease-resistant.

Selective breeding is a slow, highly uncertain process. It can take years before breeders learn if a cross was successful. Even if a new variety results, there is no assurance that it is commercially valuable. Nonetheless, there are many success stories. Among them are the "super trees" developed by Manville Corporation.

It used to take 50 to 60 years, thousands of acres, countless tons of water and lots of work to care for loblolly pines until harvest. Geneticists at Manville cross-bred seeds from selected trees to produce loblolly pines that grow 50% faster than loblolly pines in natural stands. The trees can be harvested in 30 years. This makes it possible to grow more wood on the same number of acres at lower cost. The new trees are also more resistant to insects and disease. They are straighter, have smaller and fewer limbs and have higher wood density.

Another success story involves George Ware, research director for the Morton Arboretum in Illinois. After years of cross-breeding elms he has produced more than two dozen hybrids that show promise of being resistant to Dutch elm disease—a deadly fungus disease that has destroyed most American elms. Unlike American elms, Chinese elms are resistant to the disease. Ware crossed American and Chinese elms to produce his new hybrids. The hybrids resist the disease better than American elms. Ware hopes they will also have longer life spans than American elms. The American elm has a life span of 100 years, whereas the Chinese elms live 200 to 300 years.

Cloning

A clone is an organism or a group of organisms created from a single parent. It is identical to the parent because it has exactly the same genes.

To create clones of a plant, plant breeders cut cells from the plant. The cells are placed in a laboratory container together with a special growing medium that contains all the nutrients needed by the cells. The cells grow, divide and eventually form a whole plant. Cloning allows scientists to select a desirable plant and produce as many identical copies of it as they wish.

Cloning can also begin with the seeds of a plant known to be superior. A Weyerhaeuser Company has produced douglas fir clones from seeds. A single seed can be treated and grown in special mediums to produce 30 or more seedlings. By the

SHRINKING FORESTS
The Solutions

Active reforestation is an essential part of saving our forests.

To SAVE THE WORLD'S REMAINING FORESTS, people must find ways to slow and reverse destruction. One important step is reducing demand for timber. Helpful actions include increased recycling of paper, more efficient use of lumber in construction, more efficient wood-burning stoves and better use of lumber remnants. Plantations of rapidly growing tree species also limit pressure to cut ancient forests.

Above: A carpenter frames the interior walls of a new home with metal studs. *Right:* Products made from recycled paper lessen the need to destroy existing forests and ease the total amount of garbage requiring disposal.

AMERICAN NATURALISTS

ERGRE

A RECYCLED PAPER

SIMPSON

PACKAGED IN
RECYCLED
PAPERBOARD

TO OPEN • SLIDE FINGER UNDER FLAP AND LOOSEN GENTLY

RECYCLABLE • BIODEGRADABLE
RENEWABLE RESOURCE

26 C

R 18 9 5

THIS CARTON
IS MADE FROM
RECYCLED PAPERBOARD

PROOF of PURCHASE

0   30100 00133   1
16 OZ ORIGINAL ZESTA

PROTECTING FORESTS INVOLVES WISE MANAGEMENT practices as well as research to develop improved techniques for fighting fires. New technology that can control diseased organisms and harvest trees while minimizing damage to wildlife and water resources is also crucial. One essential goal is sustained yield: The amount of timber that is harvested should not be greater than the growth rate of the forest.

Left: A firefighter works quickly to contain a raging forest fire. *Above:* Helicopters and airplanes can be used to bring special fire-dousing chemicals to the scene of a blaze.

SCIENTIFIC RESEARCH HELPS protect forests in many ways. Engineers can create automobile engines that burn fuel more efficiently and produce less air pollution. Geneticists can develop improved varieties of trees. For example, it used to take 50 to 60 years before loblolly pines (grown in the southern United States) were ready for harvest. Improved breeds have cut the harvest time by 50 percent. The new breeds are also more resistant to insects and disease, are straighter and have higher wood density.

Far left: Using a process similar to cloning, scientists can grow an entire plant from an individual cell. *Left:* An emissions testing machine displays the results of an exhaust test to an inspector.

time three of the clones from one seed were five years old, they looked like triplets. The arrangement of their branches was exactly alike. All three even had a little bend in the trunk at the same spot.

Another practice whose end result is similar to cloning has been used for centuries. It involves plant cuttings. Certain parts of some plants can be removed and placed in soil to form new plants. For example, when a branch from a willow tree is removed and put in soil, it quickly grows roots and becomes a self-sufficient plant. In some areas, cuttings have been used to develop new forests.

Biotechnology

In recent decades scientists have developed a number of ways to change a cell's genetic material. For instance, cells can be altered to produce chemicals that they would not naturally make. Biotechnology is a young, exciting and rapidly changing field. Its possibilities seem endless, limited only by the bounds of scientists' imaginations.

Using biotechnology, scientists expect to be able to develop improved breeds at a much faster pace than with traditional

A BIRD'S EYE VIEW

A colorful hot-air balloon moves slowly over the rain forest of French Guiana, on the northeastern coast of South America. The balloon is ferrying food and other supplies to a group of scientists high in the forest's canopy. The scientists are working on a platform some 130 feet (40 meters) above the ground. During the daytime, some of the scientists descend into the forest depths on rope ladders. At night, they sleep in a tent on the platform.

Adventurous scientists have developed imaginative ways to investigate forest canopies. They have built lightweight rope walkways between the crowns of trees, so they could walk among the treetops. They string rope webbing, then suspend themselves like spiders. Such techniques enable the scientists to observe forest organisms in their natural surroundings and to collect specimens for further study. The efforts of these scientists have provided much new

information on how forests work.

Scientists also go aloft in gondolas carried by hot-air balloons. They photograph canopies from ultralight aircraft and helicopters. They make use of satellites that orbit the Earth, too. Images taken by cameras aboard satellites can be used to make maps of forests. Each year, new maps can be made, helping scientists to monitor changes such as the rate of forest destruction.

cross-breeding methods. One goal of plant scientists is to create plants that use nitrogen from the air to make their own fertilizers. They hope to give plants genes that will make them resistant to certain diseases, increase the nutritional value of their fruits, or make them less susceptible to drought or pollution. They hope to insert genes that will speed a plant's rate of photosynthesis, so that the plant will grow faster.

Basically, biotechnology involves inserting a desired gene into an individual plant cell. Once the plant cell is altered in this way, it is made to divide and grow into a mature plant. Each cell in the mature plant will have a copy of the desired gene. The desired gene will carry out its function, such as directing the synthesis of a protein new to that cell. The cell will do this without losing any other important traits.

One biotechnology technique is gene splicing. In this process, a gene is removed from one organism and made part of another organism's genetic material. Sometimes the process is called recombinant-DNA because it recombines DNA in new ways.

Another technique is DNA cloning. The process can result in the production of millions of copies of a specific piece of DNA. This makes it easier for scientists to analyze the DNA's structure and study its functions. The copies could also be introduced into cells that might benefit from the information in that DNA. For example, DNA that carries instructions for resistance to a specific disease could be cloned, then introduced into trees that are susceptible to the disease.

Once the structure of a gene is known, it is possible to make copies of the gene. Special gene machines have been developed to speed the process. Gene machines are instruments that can chemically synthesize a gene from its subunits, according to programmed instructions.

One of the most recent developments in the biotechnology revolution is the creation of designer genes. These are genes that do not exist in nature. They can direct the production of chemicals that do not exist in nature. The process is often called protein engineering. Almost all the substances produced by cells are proteins, and almost all biological processes are controlled by proteins. Once scientists know the DNA structure of a gene, they can change that structure. This will change the instructions that the gene gives the cell for producing a certain protein. A new kind of protein will be produced. Scientists hope to use this technique to create proteins for specific tasks, such as fighting diseases for which there is no known cure.

In 1990, Bruce E. Haissig of the U.S. Forest Service reported that he and other scientists had used biotechnology to develop a new variety of poplar. The poplars are designed to be grown on large plantations, then harvested and used as a source of energy. One problem with growing poplars on plantations has been that young trees are often crowded out and killed by weeds. Removing weeds by hand is time-consuming and expensive. Using weedkillers hasn't worked. They often kill not only the weeds but also the poplars.

Haissig and his colleagues introduced a bacterial gene into poplar cells grown in laboratory dishes. The gene made the poplars resistant to a widely used weedkiller, glyphosate. This means that glyphosate can be used around this poplar variety without harming the trees. This will lower the cost of raising poplars on plantations.

One question remains from Haissig's work: Will the poplars pass on the weedkiller resistance to their offspring? Poplars do not flower and produce seeds until they are about 15 years old. Thus it will be around the year 2005 that this question is answered—at least for the poplars. Scientists are conducting similar work with jack pines. These trees produce seeds at a much younger age.

So far, most trees, including those that are most improtant commercially, cannot be raised from cells grown in laboratory dishes. Scientists are testing new techniques that may overcome this difficulty. Many are optimistic that during the 21st century, biotechnology will transform forestry, speeding the growth of trees that provide needed habitats for wildlife and helping to meet the needs of continually expanding human populations.

9

FORESTS FOR THE FUTURE

The concept of planting new forests for the future came into being more than 700 years ago, in the 1300s. European rulers saw that their forests were vanishing. The habitats of animals they liked to hunt were disappearing. To protect their resources, the rulers limited people's rights to cut trees. From this, it was but a short step for someone to suggest planting new trees to grow into forests for the use of the ruler.

The early European settlers in North America did not worry about shrinking forests. They thought they would never run out of wood. By the 1800s, however, people began to worry. One of the first to express concern was the author James Fenimore Cooper: "What will the axemen do, when they have cut their way from sea to sea?"

By 1920, U.S. forests had shrunk to their lowest level. People became serious about replanting. In the 1930s, lumber companies in the south began to grow conifer seedlings on a large scale in tree nurseries. They began to replant large areas that had been deforested. Among the new forests is a pine forest that covers more than 60,000 acres (24,3000 hectares) in Louisiana—one of the largest replanted forests in the world.

Private companies and organizations plus government agencies have continued to replant many deforested areas in

Opposite page: Replanting and replenishing the forests that have been stripped by human hands is the oldest, and still most immediately successful, way to combat the substantial loss of trees all over the Earth. Here, a new crop of Douglas firs thrives in Oregon.

the United States. Cities are not being ignored, either. New efforts are under way to replace the many trees that were cut down to build buildings, roads, sidewalks and parking lots. In the late 1980s, the American Forestry Association began a campaign called Global ReLeaf. Its goal was to plant 100 million trees in American cities and towns by 1992.

Other countries have also tried to reverse the effects of overcutting. The country that has been most successful has been South Korea. The Korean War of the 1950s caused extensive damage to forests. Following the war, the collection of wood to burn as fuel destroyed much of the remaining forests. The situation became so serious that in 1969 a United Nations report said, "There is a critical need for fuel for heating and cooking, which causes people to cut grass, seedlings, shrubs and tree branches, and to rake the ground of all leaves, litter and other burnable material."

In the early 1970s, the government of South Korea launched a well-organized program to reforest their country. To help build interest and support among South Koreans, the government put up billboards painted with messages such as "Love Trees, Love Your Country." Local people were involved in the program. They were shown how to plant and care for trees. They were told how they would benefit from the new forests. Soon, barren hills were covered with row upon row of young trees. Today, there are thriving forests on about one-third of the land in South Korea.

Unfortunately, many other tree planting programs have been failures. Millions of seedlings die because of lack of proper care. Millions more are eaten by livestock or cut down for firewood before they grow very tall. Other programs have been announced with lots of publicity, only to falter because of lack of money or other problems. Each failure, however, teaches us something. It helps us design better programs with better chances of success.

A Program in Nepal

Many members of the world community are helping developing nations fight deforestation and at the same time

A MODERN JOHNNY APPLESEED

Around the year 1800, a legend was born on the American frontier. A pioneer named John Chapman planted apple trees throughout the Ohio River valley and other parts of the Midwest. Every autumn, Chapman traveled the cider presses in the East. He collected the mashed residue that remained after the juice had been squeezed out of the apples. He washed the seeds out of this residue, then let them dry in the sun. The next spring, Chapman walked westward, handing out seeds to local Indians and new settlers, and stopping here and there to plant some of the seeds himself—in meadows, along rivers and anywhere else that seemed a good spot for an apple orchard. Many Indians and settlers considered Chapman a saint. They called him Johnny Appleseed.

Today, many people are imitating Chapman. One of these modern Johnny Appleseeds is Andy Lipkis. He began planting trees in 1970, when he was 15 years old and saw how the Los Angeles smog was killing trees in his summer camp in the San Bernardino mountains. He and some other campers tore up a parking lot and planted smog-resistant evergreens. Twenty years later, in 1990, the trees continued to thrive.

Lipkis realized that each individual has the power to change the environment. He formed an organization that in 1974 officially became TreePeople. Through TreePeople, Lipkis has helped other people form organizations and grow trees in their own communities. Lipkis calls these people "citizen foresters." He and his colleagues have inspired the planting of more than 200 million trees around the world—including more than 1 million trees in Southern California.

improve living standards. One example can be seen in Nepal. Scientists from Argonne National Laboratory, a research center near Chicago, are working with Nepalese citizens to raise trees. Argonne learned that many villagers had to spend three to four hours to collect enough wood to cook for three days. Another two to six hours a day were spent collecting fodder for livestock. Argonne forester Martha Avery pointed out: "As forests become depleted, the amount of time needed to collect fuel wood and fodder increases, leaving less time for agricultural activity or cottage industry."

Argonne has established three tree nurseries in the hills where most of Nepal's population is concentrated. "At peak periods, these nurseries employ more than 200 Nepalese in the production of approximately 300,000 seedlings annually," noted Avery.

Seeds and cuttings from trees valued by local Nepalese are grown in the nurseries until they are large enough to survive outdoors. Then some of the seedlings are planted in research and demonstration areas next to the nurseries. The remainder are given to people to plant on their farms or in plantation forests. Branches from the trees will be used by the Nepalese to heat homes and build fires for cooking and other purposes. Leaves will be used as fodder for cattle, water buffalo and other livestock.

In their research areas, the Argonne scientists are testing four production systems. One is a form of agroforestry, with grass and crops planted between rows of trees. Another plants rows of trees along with contours of hills, to reduce soil erosion. The remaining systems plant trees very close together, to encourage the growth of lots of branches and foliage in a short period of time. "When the nursery plantings are established, the growth of specific species and sites will be evaluated as well as the different cultivation systems," said Avery. "The fodder and fuel wood yields for the various species and cultivation systems will be determined. In addition, the economics, social implications and environmental effects of the tree production systems will be analyzed."

Looking to the Future

Nearly a century ago, U.S. president Theodore Roosevelt said, "The nation behaves well if it treats the natural resources as assets which it must turn over to the next generation, increased and not impaired in value."

Since Roosevelt's time, it has become obvious that people must look beyond the borders of their own country. They must conserve not only their own country's resources but also those of other countries. They must be concerned about pollution produced overseas as well as pollution produced by factories and automobiles in their own neighborhood. "It is now clear that the environment cannot be protected just by the actions we take in our own backyard; the health and well-being of people in one country may depend upon choices made by individuals and policymakers far from their national boundaries. Increasing numbers of people now perceive their own vested interest in international issues," noted Susan R. Fletcher, senior analyst in international environmental policy at the U.S. Congressional Research Service.

Roosevelt's words remain relevant, however. The fate of the world's remaining forests will be determined by the actions of people living today. We can continue to exploit the forests, destroying them for our immediate needs and desires. Or we can protect them for future generations. Will future generations look back and curse us for our wasteful, greedy behavior? Or will they praise us for reversing the destructiveness that has already created so many problems? The decision is ours.

GLOSSARY

acid rain Rain and other precipitation polluted by acids, particularly sulfuric acid and nitric acid.

air pollution The presence in air of acids, smoke and other materials that damage the air's quality.

biomass Wood, crop residues and other organic matter.

biotechnology the manipulation of a cell's genes so that the cell can produce new products.

canopy The upper layer of a forest, formed by the crowns (leaves and branches) of the tallest trees.

clear-cutting A forest management practice that involves cutting all the trees within an area at one time.

cloning Methods used to make copies of a gene or to obtain a group of genetically identical cells from a single cell.

combustion Burning, accompanied by the release of energy in the form of heat and light. The combustion of fossil fuels, such as oil and coal, is a basic cause of air pollution.

conifers Trees that bear their seeds in cones, such as pines, hemlocks, firs and spruce.

conservation Measures taken to protect and improve forests and other natural resources.

decomposition The breakdown of matter into simpler substances by bacteria and other means.

deciduous tree Trees that shed their leaves in the autumn, including oaks, maples, hickories and elms.

deforestation The clearing away of forests.

desertification The spread of desertlike conditions in arid and semiarid regions, often as a result of deforestation.

ecosystem All the organisms in an area and their interactions with one another and with their nonliving surroundings.

epiphyte A plant that lives upon another plant, depending on the host plant for physical support but not harming it in any way.

erosion The wearing away of soil by running water, wind and other forces.

fertilizer A nutrient added to the soil to improve plant growth.

fossil fuels Oil, coal and natural gas, formed from the remains of organisms that lived millions of years ago.

genes The units of inheritance, present in every cell, that determine the characteristics of the organism.

genetic engineering The process of inserting new genetic information into existing cells, to modify the characteristics of an organism.

greenhouse effect The absorption by gases in the atmosphere of heat energy radiated from the Earth's surface, causing the atmosphere to become warmer.

monoculture The practice of growing a single crop or type of tree in an area.

ozone a form of oxygen present primarily in the stratosphere and responsible for blocking ultraviolet radiation; concentrations near the Earth's surface contribute to smog.

rain forest A forest characterized by high amounts of precipitation.

recycling The process of using something over and over again or of converting discarded materials into new products.

reforestation Replanting previously forested areas with trees.

silt Very fine particles of soil, sand or rock carried by moving water.

smog A form of air pollution consisting of smoke and other pollutants combined with fog.

transpiration The process by which a plant eliminates excess water vapor through its leaves.

watershed The area from which water drains into a pond, lake or stream.

FURTHER READING

Berger, John J. *Restoring the Earth: How Americans Are Working to Renew Our Damaged Environment*. New York: Alfred A. Knopf, 1985.

Brown, Lester R., et al. *State of the World 1989*. New York: W.W. Norton & Company, 1989.

Collins, Mark (ed.). *The Last Rain Forests: A World Conservation Atlas*. New York: Oxford University Press, 1990.

Ervin, Keith. *Fragile Majesty: The Battle for North America's Last Great Forest*. Seattle: The Mountaineers, 1989.

Goldsmith, Edward, and Nicholas Hildyard (eds.). *The Earth Report: The Essential Guide to Global Ecological Issues*. Los Angeles: Price Stern Sloan, 1988.

Hecht, Susanna, and Alexander Cockburn. *The Fate of the Forest: Developers, Destroyers and Defenders of the Amazon*. London: Verso, 1989.

Kelly, David, and Gary Braasch. *Secrets of the Old Growth Forest*. Salt Lake City: Gibbs Smith, 1988.

Ketchum, Robert Glenn, and Carey D. Ketchum. *The Tongass: Alaska's Vanishing Rain Forest*. New York: Farrar, Straus & Giroux, 1987.

Lipkis, Andy, and Katie Lipkis. *The Simple Act of Planting a Tree: Healing Your Neighborhood, Your City, and Your World*. Los Angeles: Jeremy P. Tarcher, 1990.

Manes, Christopher. *Green Rage: Radical Environmentalism and the Unmaking of Civilization*. Boston: Little, Brown & Company, 1990.

Repetto, Robert. *The Forest for the Trees? Government Policies and the Misuse of Forest Resources*. Washington, DC: World Resources Institute, 1988.

Robinson, Gordon. *The Forest and the Trees: A Guide to Excellent Forestry*. Washington, DC: Island Press, 1988.

Salisbury, Harrison E. *The Great Black Dragon Fire: A Chinese Inferno*. Boston: Little, Brown & Company, 1989.

Steger, Will, and Jon Bowermaster. *Saving the Earth: A Citizen's Guide to Environmental Action*. New York: Alfred A. Knopf, 1990.

Weber, Thomas. *Hugging the Trees: The Story of the Chipko Movement*. New York: Penguin, 1990.

World Commission on Environment and Development. *Our Common Future*. New York: Oxford University Press, 1987.

The following periodicals regularly cover issues associated with forests and deforestation:

Amicus Journal. National Resources Defense Council, 40 West 20th Street, New York, NY 10011.

Environment. Heldref Publications, 1730 M L King Jr. Way, Berkeley, CA 94709.

Environmental Action. Environmental Action, Inc., 1525 New Hampshire, Washington, DC 20036.

Greenpeace. Greenpeace USA, 1436 U Street, NW, Washington, DC 20009.

Natural History. American Museum of Natural History, Central Park West at 79th Street, New York, NY 10024.

Science News. Science Service, Inc., 1719 N Street, NW, Washington, DC 20036.

Scientific American. Scientific American, Inc., 415 Madison Avenue, New York, NY 10017.

Sierra. Sierra Club, 730 Polk Street, San Francisco, CA 94109.

World Watch. Worldwatch Institute, 1776 Massachusetts Avenue, NW, Washington, DC 20036.

Directories of government agencies and private organizations concerned with environmental issues:

Conservation Directory. National Wildlife Federation, 8925 Leesburg Pike, Vienna, VA 22184.

Directory of Environmental Organizations. Educational Communications, Box 35473, Los Angeles, CA 90035.

Directory of National Environmental Organizations. U.S. Environmental Directories, Box 65156, St. Paul, MN 55165.

INDEX

Photo Credits

Page 4, © Robert Semeniuk/First Light, Toronto; p.10, © Grant Heilman/Grant Heilman Photography; p.19, © Claude Steelman/Tom Stack & Associates; p.22, © Grant Heilman/Grant Heilman Photography; p.34, © Grant Heilman/Grant Heilman Photography; p.43, Photo Researchers, Inc.; p.48, © Jessie Parker/First Light, Toronto; p.56, © Grant Heilman/Grant Heilman Photography; p.66, Reuters/Bettmann Newsphotos; p.69, © George H. Harrison/Grant Heilman Photography; p.74, Courtesy Dr. Brian Boom; p. 78, Gamma Liaison; p. 88, © David M. Dennis/Tom Stack & Associates; p. 100, © Grant Heilman/Grant Heilman Photography; p. 103, The Bettmann Archive.

Cover, portfolio opener/Problems, © Greenpeace/Midgley; portfolio page 2, © Thomas Kitchin/Tom Stack & Associates; portfolio page 3, Jack Swenson, Tom Stack & Associates; portfolio page 4, © Krafft-Explorer/Photo Researchers, Inc.; portfolio page 5, © Steve Elmore/Tom Stack & Associates; portfolio pages 6–7, © Doug Sokell/ Tom Stack & Associates; portfolio page 8, © Art Stein/Photo Researchers, Inc.
Portfolio Solutions: Opener, Warren Uzzle/Photo Researchers, Inc.; portfolio page 2 (left), © Hector Gonzalez; portfolio pages 2–3, © Runk–Schoenberger/Grant Heilman Photography; portfolio page 4, © U.S. Forest Service; portfolio page 5, © Brian Milne/First Light, Toronto; portfolio page 6, © David M. Dennis/Tom Stack & Associates; portfolio page 7, © Dave Davidson/Tom Stack & Associates; portfolio page 8, © Richard P. Smith/Tom Stack & Associates.

Photo Research by Photosearch, Inc.